Cretin Boy

JIM LANDWEHR

Burning Bulb
PUBLISHING

Cretin Boy
By **Jim Landwehr**

Burning Bulb Publishing
P.O. Box 4721
Bridgeport, WV 26330-4721
United States of America
www.BurningBulbPublishing.com

First Edition.

Paperback Edition ISBN: 978-1-948278-28-7

Printed in the United States of America

Dedication

This book is dedicated to my high school friends,
Pat, Pete, Dan and Doug.
Their friendship through those awkward high school years
helped to make my time at Cretin so much richer.

ACKNOWLEDGEMENTS

I'd like to thank the Mighty Monday Nighters, my writing workshop friends at AllWriters' Workplace and Workshop. Their critiques on many of these stories made them all just a little better. Thanks also to the entire Cretin class of 1979, and more specifically those on Facebook who cheered me on and helped me fact check. Guys like Jim Cunningham, Tim Godfrey, Dino Joyce, Dennis Keiger, Mike Morgan, Bill Robertson, Dave Slattery, and Mike Tomars. Though I didn't hang out with you in high school, I sure appreciate your friendship now. Of course, thanks and appreciation to my wife who understands my need to pen these thoughts, sometimes at the expense of household repairs and other obligations. To the Christian Brothers, lay teachers, nuns and military staff who taught during those four years at Cretin, I thank you for the education, guidance and patience you had with the class of 1979. You served all of us well. And, finally, I must note that this work is intended to describe my experiences at Cretin with the intent to entertain and not vilify anyone. To that end, most of the names used herein are real, though I took liberty to use aliases where I felt appropriate.

Portions of this book have previously appeared in Peninsula Pulse, Coexistence Journal, Portage Magazine and The Waif Project.

CHAPTER 1: FIVE YEAR REUNION

I am still at a loss as to why I felt compelled to attend my five year high school reunion in the summer of 1984. I had a clique of six or so close friends, but beyond that I was indifferent toward most of my classmates. The burn-outs had no appeal to me as drugs weren't really my thing. I was a fledgling athlete, so I didn't have much in common with the jocks other than my efforts from my spot on the bench. I wasn't super smart, so was discounted by the brains; I was an introvert, so a non-factor among the popular crowd. Furthermore, I was five years into a double major in Geography and Anthropology and was fairly self-conscious about that reality, as well. In truth, I had more reasons not to attend than I did to show up and revisit those awkward high school years. At the same time, I thought it might be a good chance to see some of my circle I'd since lost touch with.

The event was held at Doc's Place, a bar and party hall on Montreal in Saint Paul, the same venue at which my sister held her wedding reception a few years before. I dressed in a pair of straight leg jeans, high-topped leather sneakers, fitted shirt and a skinny tie, in the fashion of the eighties. There was a cash bar, light hors de oeuvres, and all the socializing an introvert like me could handle. I walked in and immediately gravitated in the direction of my friend group. I was grateful to find Pete Grayson and Dan Dolan sitting at a table talking, so I approached it and sat down.

"Hey guys, what's up?" I asked.

"Not too much, Jimbo. Good to see you. What's new?" Dan asked.

"Ah, nothing much. Finishing up at the U in another quarter or two. Otherwise, just working at Wards and living at home," I said, thinking myself an underachiever and capable of so much more. The guys nodded. They knew my declared majors and were cool about not mocking me for them. I dreaded answering the question from anyone in my class who didn't know me as well as my close friends. I'd had enough puzzled looks from people over the years over my unique choice in college majors. It was why I hung with these guys. They accepted me for who I was and not for who they thought I should be.

Attendance seemed really light given our class size of nearly two hundred twenty students. I wandered over to the bar and got a tap beer. It figured to be a long evening and a little liquid courage to keep me blabbering felt like a good idea. On my way back, I said hi to a few of the popular guys who knew everyone and got along with most. Making small talk with people I hadn't seen in five years was what I loathed most in the world, which was why I debated showing up in the first place.

Much like in high school, our friend groups clumped together in cliques and chatted.

"Hey, who's the Harley dude over there? I don't recognize him," I said.

"That's Chris Yorga," Pete said.

"What? Are you kidding me?"

Chris Yorga was probably the last person on earth I would have pegged for being decked out in a leather vest, jeans and a trucker's wallet hooked to a chain in his back pocket. He had long hair, was nearly a foot taller than I remembered him and sported a full beard and mustache. Five years earlier he'd been the small, geeky, nerdy kid everyone ridiculed. Most of the teasing was done in a big-brother-beating-up-little-brother sort of way. He'd been a nice enough kid, just sort of small and meek, an easy target for anyone needing to boost their own self-esteem, including myself. To see him transformed into a Harley biker dude was dumbfounding.

"Nope, go ask him," Pete said.

"I'll take your word for it," I replied.

I don't know why it struck me as so odd. People change all the time. It was just that this was such a 180 degree turn from who he was. Everyone else seemed pretty much the same. Some fatter or thinner or balder, but, for the most part, the same. Chris' transformation was a little like seeing Mr. Rogers returning to the screen to play Dirty Harry. From cardigan sweater to Magnum 44. The fact that he turned the tables on his life was a little bit liberating as well. It was the single biggest takeaway I mustered from the event. If he could remake himself in five years and be completely okay with his new identity, it meant we all could, if we wanted. And there was some comfort in that at the end of the night as I went home to resume my pursuit of who Jim Landwehr was going to be.

CHAPTER 2: ORIENTATION

I shuffled along with a lineup of forty or so other freshmen into the cramped back room known as the Quartermasters. The day before, I didn't even know what Quartermasters meant. A rare coin collecting term, perhaps? I learned it was the area where supplies were held and doled out, by the quartermaster personnel. We were all there to get our standard issue military uniforms we would be required to wear every day for the next four years of high school. Walking up and down the line of students was a gravel-voiced asshole with a crew cut, who I would soon come to know as Sergeant Stewart. He had an imposing presence and a demeanor as tough as nails.

"Now listen up, and listen good, frosh. You are here to get your military uniform you will be expected to return in good and proper condition at the end of the year. Do you understand me?"

His question was answered with a smattering of "Yes's."

"What? Did I hear that right? Yes? No, not yes. Yes, sir! You will *always* address me as sir, as well as Sergeant Stephens here, and the rest of the military faculty in this school. Do you understand, gentlemen?" Sergeant Stephens was a black gentleman standing nearby, sporting a well-trimmed mustache and dressed in a military uniform like the one we were receiving.

Half of those present answered, "Yes, sir."

Cupping his hand to his ear, Sargent shouted, "What? I can't hear you. Answer authority with authority!"

"Yes, sir!" shouted everyone in the room.

"That's better. Now you will all stay single file and take what is given to you. If your mama took down your sizes and you brought them with you, you will get a uniform that fits. If she did not, you will be measured and hopefully what you get will work out."

As the line slowly crept forward, Sergeant Stewart snapped at a couple of boys for various courtesy infractions, or for mumbling. I started to dread my turn in front of him as he manned the pants window. From where I stood, this whole military thing seemed like just a whole lot of yelling. I approached the counter and said, "I need a pair of thirty-two waist pants, sir."

"Pants? Pants? Women wear pants. They are called trousers, son!"

I stood there with my dignity on the floor wondering what to say next. "Uh, then I need a pair of thirty-two waist trousers, I guess."

He looked at me menacingly and squinted his eyes. "Are you forgetting something?"

"Not that I know of, sir."

"Sir! There it is. That's better! Now I will get you your trousers, because we don't have any pants here, young man."

"Thank you, sir," I replied in an attempt to avoid any further ego bludgeoning.

The whole exchange didn't help my unrest at being in a new school with rigid new rules and a ton of new faces around me. It was 1975 and I was here following in my Brother Tom's footsteps. He graduated from the school in 1973. The allure of his uniform and his marksmanship medals that looked so intriguing a couple of years ago was waning here in the presence of the verbal flogging being issued in the Quartermasters.

After receiving my two pairs of trousers, I continued on down the line where I was issued two finely pressed light brown dress shirts, two black neckties, a drab green trench coat and a black knit belt. Next I was measured and sized for my dress-blouse. These were the drab green blazers that displayed our class colored nametags, ranks, and any ribbons or medals we might achieve. We wore them once a week for military inspection as well as for special ceremonies, like parades.

As I was being measured, I chose not to challenge the fact that up until that moment, I was raised to understand only women and girls wore blouses, let alone dress-blouses, a double feminine reference. After the moral beat down I'd been through up to this point, they could have told me jockey shorts were called panties and I wouldn't have second guessed. I was highly gender-confused at the moment – at least from a fashion standpoint.

I finished up with a trip through the store portion of the Quartermasters where other non-issued uniform accoutrements were offered for sale. There I purchased my collar brass, which were a pair of circular pins about the size of quarters, with a decorative raised torch. Along with that, I bought a brass belt buckle, nametag and a black and gold cloth private's rank that could be snapped onto the shoulder flap of my masculine dress-blouse. For footwear, we were expected to purchase black dress shoes and black socks to finish out the uniform. One thing was sure, this military uniform required a dizzying array of accessories. By the end of the line, I wasn't sure what I'd gotten into, but when I walked out with a stack of items, I knew I was in deep.

CHAPTER 3: HOMEROOM

Homerooms at Cretin were assigned alphabetically by last name. My homeroom, 212, was filled with the L and M guys. Over my four years in high school, I got to know these classmates pretty well, at least in regards to who I wanted to hang out with. I couldn't be everyone's friend, but I got along tolerably with most everyone in the room. My desk was between Dominic Lagos, a black, six-foot soccer star, and Jim Lauer a quiet, cool kid behind me. Dominic had a propensity for facing my desk and giving me grief until homeroom started at eight o'clock. When the bell rang he'd spin back around and face the front. For some reason, he took delight in fake slapping my head and just getting in my face. It was harmless teasing, but got annoying on occasion.

Behind me, sat Jim Langston, a nice enough guy and memorable mostly for the poem he once said to me:

"I like pot
I smoke it a lot
so stop spraying it
with Paraquat."

While I never smoked pot in high school, I had to admit, his poem had a catchy rhyme and a righteous message to it.

Mr. Hughes was our homeroom teacher, also known as Hondo, his nickname as an off-hours talented magician. He was a cool teacher in his late twenties at the time who taught calculus and honors calc. I never took a class from him, mainly because I was a bit of a math flunky. A soft fog descends over me whenever numbers come into play. But from what I heard others saying, he was a great teacher who worked hard with struggling students. Furthermore, he cared deeply about his homeroom students. When he found out I'd lost my dad young, he reached out and offered to take a friend and me to a

Minnesota Twins game. He was inspired by the Big Brothers/Big Sisters program, which would explain his outreach. I took him up on his offer, and he, Pete, myself and one of Hondo's friends went and had a great time. It meant a lot to me that he cared enough to extend such a gracious invitation.

As mentioned, Hondo also had an alter-ego as Hondo the Magician. He had wickedly good magic skills. Every once in a while in homeroom, we convinced him to do a trick before class started. He was amazing with his card tricks and was capable of wowing us with a silver dollar that started in his palm and emerged from his elbow, or out of a student's ear. He was so adept at it, he did shows on the side, as a little supplemental income to go with his teaching. Once he retired, he made quite a successful career as an entertainer and magician. He met quite a few professional sports stars and celebrities along the way, including Muhammed Ali and Paul Molitor.

***

One of the distinct memories from Hondo's homeroom came during one of the school-wide fundraisers every year, the SPAFF festival. The acronym stood for, Students, Parents, Alumni, Faculty and Friends. During SPAFF drives, all students were encouraged to sell tickets for a raffle featuring a number of donated prizes. As part of every homeroom's team-building efforts, there were lighthearted competitions between rooms over which one could raise the most money. And to help foster sales, every year we were fed the line that if we went door-to-door dressed in our military uniforms, we would probably have better luck selling tickets than if we were wearing our street clothes.

Well, about the last thing I wanted to do after a long day at school in a military uniform was to walk the streets of my neighborhood in that same uniform, peddling raffle tickets. The expectation that I would ask complete strangers to buy raffle tickets seemed like a form of torture for an introvert like me. Instead, I resorted to the more desperate sales technique of begging family members to take the burdensome tickets off my hands. To make matters worse, every year our homeroom adopted the goal of trying to get each student to sell at least fifty dollars of SPAFF tickets, at a dollar a piece.

Despite my valiant sales efforts, I struggled to sell tickets, so I started buying them with my own money. I had a decent job so, during my upperclassmen years, I bought as much as thirty dollars' worth. It was part laziness, part not wanting to let my teacher and classmates down. So, I filled them out with my own name and address, with the thought I might actually win one of the prizes as kind of a bonus to my whole self-imposed SPAFF bailout.

As it turned out, Mr. Hughes was doing some sort of stub review as gatekeeper for our homeroom's effort toward the dollar goal. He approached me one morning near the end of the SPAFF drive.

"Hey, Jim. I was looking at some of the ticket stubs, and I couldn't help but notice many of them have your name on them. I just wanted to make sure you intended to do that, and you're not doing it because you're feeling pressured by our homeroom goal."

"Uh, no, not at all. I bought them with my own money because I want a chance to win one of the prizes," I lied.

"Are you sure? Because I don't want you to feel obligated."

"Oh, no, I totally wanted to do this." The lies spilled forth like a severed artery.

"Okay, buddy. Just checking. Great job reaching your goal. Keep selling and we'll see how much we can do as a homeroom."

Ironically enough, I capped out at exactly fifty dollars. I secretly hated the over achievers in class who sold more than a hundred dollars' worth, earning them special recognition on the tally board. I looked at my outlay of cash for SPAFF as a sort of once-a-year "student fee." The extent of my SPAFF efforts stopped soundly at the letter S. The fundraiser was one of those things I didn't always agree with but just had to do. Perhaps the best takeaway of the whole experience was the lesson that I was not cut out for a career in sales. And, to add insult to injury, when the final raffle names were called, I didn't win a thing.

CHAPTER 4: FRIENDS

High school brings a whole lot of change to a young person's life, obviously. For starters, there is the hormonal onslaught of puberty. Acne, body hair and deepening voices are just the tip of the teenage iceberg. Throw into that mix the elements of peer pressure, a yearning for independence and the endless longing for acceptance and fitting in, and you have a period of life unlike any other. Furthermore, kids are thrust into a new building with hundreds of new faces after years of being with a group they had carved out their niche with. It is a time of radical life change. It's no wonder teenagers get such a bad rap for being moody and angsty.

Because I was a shy kid, the first few weeks of school were difficult. I knew a few of the guys from the freshman football team, but, being one of the smallest guys on the team and a bench warming second stringer, I didn't really develop any as close friends. Like every kid though, eventually I found a group of friends I would hang out with for the duration of our four years together at Cretin.

For starters, there was Pat Judd, a kid I'd known from the eighth grade football team. A good looking guy, blond and slim, I still consider him one of my best lifetime friends. We grew up three blocks from each other, and something about our senses of humor just clicked. He and I played together on the Junior Varsity soccer team sophomore year and we both worked at the Lexington restaurant for a couple of years while at Cretin.

Pat struggled with high school from a social standpoint. He worked too much and too late at night and always claimed he was "in a slump" for much of his high school years. High school does different things to different people. Despite our contrasting memories of our days at Cretin, he was fun to be around and his wit was infectious. We regularly joked about our hair looking bad at the most inopportune time around girls, in a day when hair was everything. Our shared sense of humor was the strongest of many points of connection between us, so best friends we became.

Pete Grayson was another of those close friends in my circle. These were the ones I could confide in, who understood me and my quirks, guys who I spent most of my time with. Like Pat, Pete also lived three blocks away from me, albeit on Summit Avenue, a boulevard lined with homes of wealthy families. Pete was a shorter guy with dark curly hair that went rogue in the summers when the heat and humidity turned his head into a cocklebur. Like the rest of us, he had a wicked sense of humor. Pete's shorter stature led him to label me with the nickname Tree. I'd been called worse things, so Tree was actually sort of endearing.

His house was a favorite hangout for us, in part because of his basement pool table and a spacious driveway with a basketball court. I remember hanging out there one day when he asked, "Hey, Jim, you want a hot dog for lunch?"

"Oh, you don't have to go to all that trouble," I said.

"It won't take more than a half a minute."

"What? That's impossible."

"No it's not. Just watch."

He went to the refrigerator and grabbed a couple of hot dogs. He put them on a plate and put them into this box called a microwave. I'd never seen one, so was skeptical, to say the least. I knew hot dogs had to be fried, boiled or grilled, all of which would take a few minutes. Pete pushed 30 seconds and then the start button. The light in the magic box went on and we watched the hot dogs spin in circles on the carousel.

When the timer bell rang, Pete popped the door open and retrieved the plate. Heat steamed off the hot dogs as he placed them onto a couple of buns. I bit into mine and nearly scorched my mouth. "Holy cats, that's hot!" I said.

"Told you, man."

"That is a fricken miracle of technology right there!" I exclaimed. It seemed like culinary witchcraft, what I just witnessed. I was amazed something could be cooked so thoroughly without any apparent heat source. No fire, no red coils, just some sort of magical, invisible waves. I remember thinking that life as we know it would never be quite the same. In this case, my enlightenment had come because Pete's family was an early adopter of this brand new technology. A year later, at great expense, our family would have one of our own, a monstrously heavy beast of a machine, but a magic box, nonetheless.

One of the other good friends of mine was Dan Dolan, a quiet kid who'd also been on the eighth grade football team with Pat and me and so eventually gravitated our way in those early months of freshman year. Like the rest of us, Dan was a solid B+ student, focused on his studies but also a distractible, risk-taking teen. His father owned Dolan's Marine, a successful boating store in downtown Saint Paul where Dan spent most of his weeknights at the store selling boating supplies and arranging mechanical service. This affiliation meant he always drove a truck with a hitch for pulling boats. His big green truck blaring Boston, Steely Dan and The Alan Parsons Project from the cassette player was the source of many rides home from school over the years. He was a good friend.

The other kid in my core group was Doug O'Malley. I originally met him as we both tried out for the freshman track team and later the junior varsity soccer team. He was a red-headed, fair-skinned guy who was extremely proud of his Irish heritage. Doug lived in Roseville, a suburb a few miles outside of Saint Paul. He came from a conservative Catholic background, but wasn't outside of pushing the boundaries of the law from time to time. For the most part, each of us was the "good kid" in our families but we were also intent on smashing the mold we'd been poured into. High school seemed the perfect place to do just that.

Pat, Pete, Dan and Doug were the guys I would consider my core group. The rest of my supporting cast of classmates were just bit players during my tenure at Cretin. One of the important functions of high school is the friends it puts in your path, some of whom remain there for a lifetime, some who drift. But these four characters made my high school years memorable and fun, and I am lucky to have had them. None of us was perfect, far from it. But when the chips were down, and you needed someone to talk to or hang out with, they were there. They had my back and I, theirs, as we struggled together through our collective coming of age. Forty years later, I still keep in contact with three of them, so the bonds we forged were strong.

CHAPTER 5: TYPING

Cretin was a college-prep school. I'm not sure they even call high schools "college prep" anymore. Frankly, if any high school is not prepping kids for college they're probably doing it wrong. As part of Cretin's college-prep curriculum, they offered a typing class elective. Mine was taught by Brother John. He was a big guy with one leg amputated below the knee. He got around on crutches and his demeanor was amiable and easygoing. I think anyone who has to listen to a roomful of manual typewriters clacking away at twenty different speeds deserves a medal of valor, so his calm persona was a perfect fit.

The typing lab was equipped with rows of Olivetti manual typewriters. I'm pretty sure these machines singlehandedly ushered in the era of carpal tunnel syndrome. We really had to hammer on the keys to get them to strike the paper hard enough to create clean, clear typeface on the page. It took deliberate effort. Electric typewriters were around at the time, but it seemed the actual purchase of them was a budgetary hit the school just wasn't ready to take. I remember leading a tour of parents through the typing lab one evening as part of an open house event. As they filed into the room, there were a few snickers when they saw the lineup of our aging word bangers. While I understood their cynicism, I also took just a little bit of offense. This was my school after all, and I took pride in it. If manual typewriters were good enough for my mom's generation, they were good enough for me. Heck, they built character.

Since listening to twenty manual typewriters clicking away for fifty minutes straight could be tedious, Brother John allowed us to bring in any record albums we might want to listen to. He used a phonograph right out of the early '60s, big and heavy with a needle that was more like a railroad spike than a stylus. Those of us who were music buffs listened to records on turntables with expensive styluses that cost more than the entire phonograph.

Because no one wanted their precious albums subjected to the abuses laid forth by the ancient monaural beast, one of the only albums that ever made it into the classroom was someone's copy of Kansas' *Point of Know Return*. Kansas was a contemporary band with a unique rock sound featuring a shrieky Hammond organ and an accompanying violin. The band was one of those you either loved or hated. A year earlier, I'd acquired a taste for the band and purchased the album for my collection, which I grew to love.

Until Brother John started playing it in typing class, that is.

Brother John played the album in virtually every class for the entire semester. Sometimes he even played one side twice over the span of a single class period. After a few weeks, the title track began to wear on me. Between the repeated plays and the repetition of the tune, the hours spent with hands on the home row became arduous. Clickety, clack, clickety, clack accompanied by the shrieking lyrics;

> *"…Was it you that said, "How long, how long,*
> *How long to the point of know return?"*

After a few weeks of this album on repeat, all I cared about was *how long to the point of dismissal from typing?* I didn't want to be "in Kansas" anymore. I don't know why no one objected more to the repeated plays, but I think the collective thought was that some music was better than no music. Another one of the irritating songs was, "Dust in the Wind." The chorus repeats over and over that "All we are is dust in the wind." It is a hauntingly morose acoustic ballad. The song is about as uplifting as its title. After hearing it every day for a semester, it made me wonder why I had to learn to type forty words per minute if all we were was just dust in the wind? It seemed kind of pointless, really. By the end of the semester, I was so sick of the album I vowed to never listen to my copy of it again.

But I typed on anyway, seemingly, to the point of no return.

CHAPTER 6: SHOOTING

As part of our military class freshman year, we were required to take a module on weapons safety, training and operation. It was here I was taught that the wartime weapon of the day was an M16, a magazine fed, shoulder fired, gas cooled, semi-automatic weapon with a maximum effective range of 550 meters. Why I continue to memorize these facts eludes me, but I do. I'd have been better served to remember how to convert a decimal to a fraction, but, alas, everyone retains something different from their high school experience.

After a couple of weeks learning about gun safety and operation in a classroom, we were taken to the rifle range to do a little sharpshooting. On that day, Sergeant Lindgren led our freshman class to the range in the basement of the main hall. When we walked in, the air smelled of gunpowder, brass and violence. It was a musty, dimly-lit room with half a dozen shooting alleys. At the end of each, a target hung on a pulley system that allowed for easy retrieval.

At the outset, Sergeant Lindgren reminded us of the golden rule of gun handling. "Remember gentlemen, treat all guns with the respect due a loaded gun," he declared. This is without a doubt the most relevant piece of advice I've retained from my four years in military class. I have a deep seated fear of guns but carry with me the fact that one can never be too careful with *any* gun.

Sergeant went on to instruct us that we would be shooting from three different positions for the day's drills; standing, kneeling and prone. Each had their own difficulties and purpose, but I was soon to discover none of it mattered. It would be revealed I was neither a sharpshooter nor destined to be on the front lines of any branch of service, except perhaps to serve as a human shield for the guy behind me. A human warning shot for retreat. I would certainly serve as no credible threat to the enemy.

The first lineup of students took their posts and were given their weapons. The rifles we used were .22 caliber, single-shot, bolt action guns that seemed to be constructed entirely out of lead. They were heavy, unwieldy things, products of some sort of cold war give-back program. They had sights on the stock and barrel, but by the end of my turn behind the trigger one would never know they actually served a purpose.

We were each given a pair of sound muffling headphones. As we lined up for the prone position, sergeant instructed us as to how to balance the gun on our non-dominant hand with our elbow as a solid base. After we positioned ourselves, he gave the word, and we began blasting away. Despite the ear protection, each shot fired on either side of me made me flinch. The same held true for my own shots. All early indications seemed to point to the fact that I was shell-shocked and I wasn't even in battle.

I tried to remember the five steps we'd learned in lecture earlier in the year. We were taught that to be an effective shooter you needed to remember the acronym BRASS. It was a commonly known acronym used by riflemen and hunters as part of their training. It stands for Breathe, Relax, Aim, Slack, Squeeze. As I fired away, my technique more closely resembled, Blink, Repeat, Approximate, Stiffen, Son-of-a. That was my progression. As I lay there on my stomach squeezing off shots of approximation and hopelessness, I realized I was not experiencing the sort of adrenaline rush I'd hoped for when I heard we were going to get to shoot a gun. Rather, the whole thing was stressful and annoying.

After shooting from the prone position, we switched to kneeling. In this posture, the shooter's elbow is placed on the knee while the shooter rests his weight on his other leg. I found this position to be even less stable for me than prone. I looked down the gun barrel through the sights and tried to focus on the bull's-eye taunting me fifty feet away. My breathing and anxiety made zeroing-in ridiculously difficult. The gun barrel seemed to take on a circular orbit winding in concentric rings around the bull's-eye. I timed my shots for when the barrel passed closest to it. To be honest, I was just winging it. I might have done as well blindfolded. After a couple more shots of flailing recklessness, I just wanted the whole exercise to be over.

With kneeling completed, we moved on to the final position, standing. I was about to discover just when I'd thought a shooting position couldn't get any more difficult, I would be introduced to one that was. Despite a rigid stance with my arms braced into my hip bones for support, I still couldn't keep the barrel from its bob and weave. It looped and zig-zagged, bent on making me look bad. Eventually I squeezed the trigger, when my wide circles narrowed to slightly smaller circles. I was suffering from some sort of low-grade PTSD and gave up caring what my score would be.

When the last shot was fired, we all handed in our ear protection, were shown our targets and our attendant scores. After looking at my scores, Sergeant Lindgren said, "Son, you will probably be well served to take a desk job if you ever enlist." I certainly couldn't argue with his evaluation. It was probably not a bad strategy considering selective service was mandatory at the time. And, while I was a horrible shot, I was not alone among my peers. My friend Pat was such a bad shot he actually hit the target of the kid next to him. I might have had a few complete target misses, but I never achieved Pat's feat. It was admirably afoul.

Over time, my shooting skills did not improve. On a hunting trip with Dan Dolan during our college years, I once saw a pheasant hiding in some snow cover.

"Hey, I got a bird here. Should I blast it?" I asked Dan.

"No, no! You've got to give it a chance. You have to flush it out, then shoot it," he said, making his way toward me.

So I raised my gun up and started walking toward the bird, in an attempt to scare it up. When I was less than three yards away, the bird took flight, spooking me much like the shots in the rifle range so many years before. I fired and, despite having a complete head start on an actual kill, I managed to only wing the poor bird. It flopped to the ground and started to run. At this point I was trigger-happy and eager to score my first pheasant. I certainly wasn't going to let it get away, so I shot again, winging it a second time. It lay there flopping around both taunting me and trying to will itself another day of life. I raised my gun up and prepared to shoot a third time before Dan stopped me.

"Whoa, whoa. Hold up there, cowboy!" he said.

"What? It's still trying to run. I don't want it to get away."

"Yeah, but do you want to eat a bird full of lead?" He then walked up to the pheasant, picked it up and wrung its neck. The bird flopped and kicked while feathers flew during Dan's mercy killing. After a few seconds the thrashing stopped and I had my first pheasant kill. Later that evening as I cleaned my bird, I discovered the plucking and dressing-out of the bird were enough to convince me that hunting was not for me. The early morning wakeup calls and my dreadful marksmanship had significant roles in my decision, as well. Fishing has always been more my speed.

Years later in 2006 I had another chance to see if age and maturity had sharpened my shooting skills. During a trip in northern Minnesota, my brother Tom asked if I wanted to do some trapshooting. He'd brought along a twelve gauge and some clay pigeons, and, while I hadn't shot a gun in twenty-five years, I thought, how hard can it be? I set up to the side of a corn field and Tom stood off to my right with the clay pigeon thrower.

"You ready, Jim?"

"Yep, launch away," I replied.

Tom chucked one into my field of view and I fired. Kablam! Miss. He flung another. Kablam! Another miss. On and on it went like this for about ten straight before I said, "Hey, I feel bad you're wasting all these pigeons on a hack like me. You take a turn."

Tom laughed at my futility. I gave him the gun, and we switched places. I walked to where he was throwing and starting flinging pigeons into his horizon. With single shots each time, he consistently turned them to powder. It was amazing to witness. He'd been hunting his whole life and was a dead-eye. At Cretin, he medaled multiple times as a marksman sharpshooter and those skills carried well into adulthood.

After he pulverized a dozen clays, he gave the gun back to me. Then he flung half a dozen more out while I whaled away with the twelve gauge, missing every one. Tired of flinging his targets into the field unscathed, Tom ambled over with a grin on his face and said, "Let's try something different." He went over and propped a couple on a large rock about twenty yards away from me. I sighted my first one and squeezed the trigger. Kablam! Miss. I missed a second time before I finally hit a target. Tom let out a cheer. It was an unnecessary reminder we were at widely different skill levels when it came to shot and powder.

Like any pursuit, perhaps if I had kept at it, I could have been a decent shot. But shooting a gun never did much for me. As I mentioned, I was never crazy about the dangers involved. That's not to say I didn't learn something in my military sharpshooting class. Between the safety awareness and my general dislike of guns, I've successfully avoided shooting myself or blowing off extremities for my whole life. I count that as a win. Suffice it to say, I never enlisted and

I've worked that desk job Sergeant Lindgren recommended, pretty much my entire life. And I think we're a better country for it.

CHAPTER 7: HAIR

It seems like an oddly vain and superficial gripe, but a big part of the whole Cretin military experience I really disliked was the short hair requirement. After all, this was the late '70s when hair was king, to say nothing of beards and mustaches. There were television stars like Farrah Fawcett and John Travolta and rock stars with flowing locks like Robert Plant and full-on afros like Lindsey Buckingham. Long hair was in, and when you're a teen, so much of your self-image is tied to your hair. And, if self-image is locked to your locks, short hair takes that advantage away.

Cretin's military standards called for no hair touching the ears or the collar of your shirt in back. If it did, you were given a demerit during inspection on Monday morning. I was a rule follower, so the thought of a demerit put fear into my heart and was cause for keeping my hair trimmed regularly. Because haircuts were an additional expense for Mom, she invested in a set of electric clippers and employed the novice barbering skills of my brother Tom to keep me shaped up.

This also put fear into my heart.

Every few weeks when the need for a Sunday night trim rolled around, Tom fired up the clippers and set to work. He often joked about cutting my hair after a few Pabst Blue Ribbons. Thankfully, he spared me by never actually carrying out the threat. Sometimes though, his cuts took on the look of someone who'd had a few beers. Tom was gifted at working power tools around the house, but hair clippers were not one of them.

We typically set up the makeshift barbershop in the kitchen. I sat in a kitchen chair rimmed by newspapers and he stood and circled me with the clippers. The small talk we made was not what you would find in your average barber shop.

"Heh, heh. How about some whitewalls, Jimbo?" he'd joke.

"Nooooo!" I replied.

"C'mon, they're all the rage right now."

"Stop, noooo!"

Whitewalls in the barber trade are created when the hair is cut above the ears enough to reveal a half inch of skin between your ears and your hair. They were a condition to be avoided. While they might look great on a '74 Cadillac, they were the antithesis of cool in the world of personal grooming. Short hair was bad enough. If you had whitewalls, you may as well check into the seminary and be done with it. Women have no love for this look, justifiably so.

There was one instance where Tom managed to give me a pretty good set of them and, of course, I was mortified. Every school day on my walk to my hitchhiking corner, I passed a cute girl who I had a crush on. She had the most beautiful smile and, when we passed, we always said hello to one another. On the morning after my whitewall cut, I passed her and covered my head in embarrassment. She laughed and kept walking without having to ask what I was doing. She knew. They all knew.

When I got to school, there were plenty of guys to remind me my barber was a hack. Comments like, "Did someone cut your hair with a weed whacker, Landwehr?" were the norm. Guys are so ruthless at that age. It didn't help when I explained to them that it was my brother.

Such were the hair woes of a teen growing up in the era of Foghat, Peter Frampton and Kiss. The irony was, throughout my entire high school tenure, I only wanted to have long hair. By the time I graduated, I grew my hair out only to discover shorter hair was coming back in. In my case, there was no justice in the world of personal grooming.

CHAPTER 8: INSPECTION

Monday at Cretin was inspection day. During our military class periods we formed our platoons in the gymnasium and underwent a uniform inspection. These were tedious exercises consisting of an upper-class officer and an assistant henchman walking from student to student in each platoon, looking for violations to the uniform and personal presentation code. I recognize it is part of the whole military training, but at the time it seemed tedious.

In these face-to-face encounters with each cadet, the officers inspected caps, collar brass, belt buckles and shoes for a sparkling shine. They also looked for uniform trousers and blouses to be pressed and clean, and hair to be cut above the ears and not touching the collar in back. Black ties were to be cinched up to the choking point, completely hiding the top button. Our tan dress shirts required a pocket protector with our nameplate and current rank attached. To finish, there were black socks and white gloves. It was all part of the complete military package.

With the exception of the "Military Joes," - those guys that were really into the military power trip - Monday morning inspections were dreaded by the rest of us during our Cretin experience. Or, maybe it was just me. I always feared getting "gigged" for having something out of line on my uniform. A gig, also known as a demerit, served as a sort of minor grade penalty. Get enough of them and they lowered your military class grade. For all but the most unkempt or rebellious it was easy enough to avoid these gigs. Take care of your appearance, look sharp and you were fine. The fear and public shaming behind the demerit system bred into us a discipline of preparation and personal appearance we might not have otherwise received as teenagers. Looking back, I guess I'm grateful for that.

This isn't to say there weren't a few military slobs. These guys rocked the rumpled look with pride. They walked around sporting any combination of wrinkled shirts, scuffed or untied shoes, and uncinched neckties. Our wool trousers required dry cleaning, and judging from the looks of some guys' pants, a few went for long periods between dry cleanings. I guess there were probably slobs at every public school, but it stood out more at Cretin where you were expected to look good.

That's not to say those of us who cared about our appearance didn't have a few military hacks to make inspection day a little easier. One well-known secret was the brass lacquer trick. When you were issued your collar brass and belt buckle at the Quartermasters store, it came sealed with a layer of lacquer to keep it from tarnishing before being sold. We were instructed to boil it in water or use Brasso© polish to take the lacquer off. The problem was, removing it meant the brass would have to thereafter be shined every week. If you left the lacquer on, though, you could get away with a month or two of no polishing. When the lacquer was eventually nicked or scratched, the shinier brass underneath it became visible and suddenly the jig was up. Inspectors could pick this out from a mile away and would tell the cadet to make sure it wasn't there the following week. In some cases, the Military Joes even gigged guys for it. They were soldier wannabes on a power trip, looking for a promotion.

The other inspection hack was chloroform shoes. By my junior year, I was tired of the weekly hassle of shoe shining. Our day-to-day black footwear took a beating and they were a pain to shine every week. As a way to skirt the system, I'd seen a couple of guys around school with chloroform shoes and was envious. These shoes are highly polished and retain the shine indefinitely. They were expensive and are typically used with tuxedos and for military dress uniforms. As I looked at it, for only fifty dollars, I would never have to shine another shoe for the next two years. It was a no brainer.

I bought a pair downtown at a store known for selling expensive brands like Florsheim, a producer of quality wing tips. To say I was the envy of my friends is an understatement. Pat and Pete were both a little jealous of my shoes. On several occasions I loaned them to my friends for their inspections. "Hey, Landwehr, can I borrow your inspection shoes?" was the Monday morning question on a weekly basis. Of course, the inspecting officers knew mine were once-a-week shoes, but there was nothing they could do about it. A pair of well-shined oxfords were all they were looking for. After graduation, I sold them to another Cretin student for half of what I paid helping, the next generation skirt the system. Those shoes were a labor saving purchase for me, and I managed to help a few friends out along the way.

CHAPTER 9: MARCHING

It was tradition at Cretin before the varsity homecoming football game every year, the freshman class marched in full dress uniform in front of the stands. In preparation our military class met on the practice football field one or two days a week in the fall, prepping for the game. This meant forming up in our ranks structured much like the real army. Six boys to a squad, four squads to a platoon, a variable number of platoons to a company, companies to battalions and battalions to a schoolwide brigade. From a leadership standpoint, there were squad leaders, platoon leaders, company and battalion commanders. The head of the whole brigade was the Cadet Colonel, the highest ranking student in the school.

So we gathered out on the practice football field in our uniforms. In the cool fall weather, our standard-issue military trench coats were permitted, along with our thin white dress gloves. There were always situations where a guy forgot his white gloves at home and used tube socks as a quick substitute in parades and during field marching, where no one noticed from afar. While the trench coats helped keep out the frosty temps, the gloves did little to warm our hands. The sergeants didn't like the students putting their hands in their coat or pants pockets and routinely yelled at us. "Quit playing pocket pool," they'd yell. I don't really know what the big deal was. Military decorum with a dash of sadism, I suppose. Evidently, discomfort built character.

After we were all lined up in our tidy rows and columns, Sergeant Stephens started barking commands our way.

"Company, ten hut!"

The entire class snapped their heels together, our feet forming a forty-five degree angle, shoulders pulled back and gazes straight forward. Sergeant Stephens used a whistle to signal the two drummers to begin serving up a marching beat, rhythmic and methodic. The snare drummer provided a catchy rat-a-tat-tat while the over-the-shoulder bass drummer thumped away a steady foot-dropping cadence.

Stephens shouted, "Company, mark time."

The entire collective began marching in place to the rhythm of the bass drum.

"Company, forward march! Leyeft, leyeft, leyeft, right, leyeft."

As we marched around the field, boys occasionally fell out of step. The only way to correct this was to execute a little skip-step to get back into sync with the rest of the company. This always made the person stand out from the rest of the group as they clomped along in elegant synchronicity. The skip-step made their head bob noticeably above the others. Viewed from a distance, it was the marching equivalent to whack a mole.

On occasion, the out of step guy inadvertently stepped on the heel of the guy in front of him, sometimes causing their heel to fall out of their shoe. We called this "getting a flat," the equivalent of a car tire flopping after getting punctured. Sometimes, the jerks in the class intentionally gave flats to other students, mostly because that's what jerks do.

Sergeant Stephens often led us in songs to keep us in time as we marched along. The songs were echoed back by the students.

"Everywhere we go *(Echo)*
People wanna know *(Echo)*
Who we are *(Echo)*
Where we come from. *(Echo)*
Where we goin' *(Echo)*
So we tell them *(Echo)*
We are Cretin *(Echo)*
Mighty, mighty Cretin" *(Echo)*

Because this song was drilled into my head, I can't seem to un-hear it. It fills critical space in my brain needed for remembering things like the PIN number for my credit card, or what I went into the kitchen to do. I credit learning how to march in formation for this undesired, lifelong earworm. My resentment is real.

On the eve of the homecoming game, all the freshman assembled in full dress uniform on the track surrounding the nearby Saint Thomas College football facility. Because our campus didn't have a varsity football field, Saint Thomas was technically our home turf. We lined up in formation behind the Color Guard which was set to lead us. They held their long flagstaffs at a forty five degree angle, tucked into a belted holder situated belly-button high, a location that was nothing short of suggestive. Of course, among the squirrely ranks of freshman there was a running joke about the phallic nature of the flagpoles carried by the Color Guard. We referred to the Guidon Bearers as the Hard-on Bearers. The mere thought alone was a completely dishonorable inference, but we are talking about fifteen-year-old boys here. The mention of it always stirred murmurs of laughter rippling through the ranks. If nothing else, it was a decent way to loosen us up before the big moment.

Over the course of the week leading up to the parade we heard rumors the opponent's fans sometimes threw things at the freshmen, so we didn't really know what to expect. When the drum beat started, Sergeant Stephens barked commands as we marked time. We tromped forward and eventually reached the main grandstand. I felt a mixture of awkwardness and school pride as we stepped in time to the beat. As we passed the crowd, they were courteous and respectful. They applauded politely as we passed in our orderly chaos, the occasional skip-stepper struggling to get back into cadence.

While it was kind of cool being in the limelight, I really just wanted to be a civilian student in the stands. Afterwards, we were all allowed to watch the game and, despite our military show of excellence, the football team went on to get soundly beaten by the visiting Burnsville Braves. In the end, the homecoming football march was every freshman's indoctrination into the military pomp and circumstance of Cretin High. On this night, we did it with near perfection and a great deal of class.

CHAPTER 10: POP CULTURE

As impressionable teens, the entertainment culture of the late seventies had an obvious impact on our intellect and behavior. The adolescent years are formative and fluid, and music, movies and television pretty much determine what kids eat, buy and listen to. For myself, music was my jam. I was never big on watching TV. I was much happier with my headphones on, listening to albums and cassette tapes. I was a huge fan of groups like Electric Light Orchestra (ELO), The Cars and Supertramp.

For a time in early 1977, I couldn't get enough of ELO. It was nothing short of obsessive idolization. Their sound was so unique. In 1977, at the zenith of their popularity, they released a double album titled, *Out of the Blue*. I bought it right away and proceeded to play it to death. When the band announced a tour to promote the album I was ecstatic. Unlike many of my friends, I had never been to a rock concert, so the day the tickets went on sale, I immediately bought one.

One ticket. For myself. Alone.

I realize that makes me sound incredibly desperate and like a total loser. But when I asked the one friend I thought might be interested in going along, and he said no, I decided I would not miss my chance. I was a huge fan, so the thought of seeing them live made me nothing less than giddy.

The ticket buying process in the late '70s involved standing in line for hours with two hundred other people outside Dayton's Department Store on the morning tickets went on sale. Then, when the doors opened I ran with the pack to get to the ticket window. When we all arrived, I stood for another hour waiting my turn. It was not unusual that despite your attempts, by the time you got to the teller, there was nothing left but tickets in the nosebleed section.

So I stood there patiently with the other ELO fans waiting to see what was left for tickets. The show was to be held at the world's worst acoustic arena, the Saint Paul Civic Center. The venue was a hockey and basketball arena first, with concerts falling into the, "*Yeah, I guess we could have concerts, too,*" category. It was so bad, the Minneapolis punk band The Replacements wrote a song about the place and titled it, "Headache." The song lyrics complain that for eight dollars and fifty cents they bought a headache. It is a statement that was not far off. The building was a gigantic, concrete and steel echo chamber. It wasn't exactly Carnegie Hall.

When I got to the window the clerk asked me how many tickets I wanted. "One please, the best available."

"Just one?" she asked with raised eyebrows.

It was a look that came just short of saying the loser window was the next one down the line. I'm sure I wasn't the first person to buy a single ticket for a concert, but it certainly felt it. Regardless, this was a concert I wasn't going to miss. I would have brought a note from my mom if it was required. Ultimately, my love for the band outweighed what *anyone* thought.

"Yes, please, the best available," I reiterated.

The clerk pitied me and was kind enough to give me an aisle seat, so I only had a stranger on one side of me.

The night of the show, I dressed in my favorite pair of corduroy Levis and a t-shirt. I hopped into Mom's Plymouth Volare' and headed downtown. On my way to the arena, I flicked the AM radio between KDWB and WDGY, the two local rock stations, in hope of stumbling upon an ELO song to get me warmed up. The volume knob crackled every time you adjusted it, and was one of the many annoying features of the Volare'. It was a drive of great anticipation, taking part in my first rock concert. When I reached the arena, I parked on a side street a few blocks away and started making my way toward it.

At the gate, I showed my ticket and passed through all the security protocol. Inside I wandered among the masses in the wide concourses of the Civic Center. At sixteen, I was still too young to buy beer, and too innocent to smoke weed. From what I saw and smelled around me, those intoxicants were standard issue for the majority of the fans. I didn't need mind altering chemicals though, because I was absolutely jittery with excitement to see my favorite group at the pinnacle of their fame. I'd heard their performance involved a stage that was a model of the spaceship on the *Out Of The Blue* album cover, which added a level of anticipation. To me, they could have played standing on shipping pallets and I would have been there.

As it turned out, the spaceship stage was not part of this show. It was used at other venues, but evidently Minnesota didn't make the cut. Regardless, when the first notes of "Standin' in the Rain" rang out, they hit me like a sonic kick in the chest. The thunderous bass and drums made my fillings rattle. The dazzling lights cut through the darkness and the crowd of 17,000 stood up and roared. It was an audiovisual spectacle unlike anything I'd ever seen. Jeff Lynne, the lead singer in his trademark Foster Grant sunglasses, stood center stage playing guitar and singing. He was the ultimate cool rock star. He was flanked on both sides by the supporting cast of players cranking out notes creating a wall of sound.

The concert rocked from hit to hit. When the first lasers shot from the floor to the ceiling and remained there shimmering, the crowd erupted. Lasers were a cutting-edge technology at the time, at least in the entertainment world. The thin blue pillars of brilliance crisscrossed the arena and lent an air of futurism to the whole spectacle. Next, the beams switched directions rapidly from their source on the floor, jutting in three different directions and twitching recklessly up to the ceiling. I'd never seen a laser light show before, so it took me by complete surprise.

The whole scene was an exercise in sensory overload. Between the lasers, the deafening music, the smell of stale beer, sweat and weed, it was a teenage ride to the gates of heaven. The band clicked through all the great songs. With the exception of a couple of awkward violin and cello solos sprinkled through the set, it was phenomenal. At the same time, it was an audiologist's nightmare. Loud. Over the top loud! I would still go as far as to say it is the loudest concert I've ever been to. But I sat there, ears bleeding, in complete ecstasy.

After a two-plus hour show, the house lights finally came up and I filed up the stairs and out of the arena with the throngs of fans. With my ears still ringing, I was musically sated and completely content. The band had not disappointed and one thing was sure, I was a rock concert convert. I'd always been a music buff, but seeing it live took it to another dimension. It was the start of a lifelong commitment to seeing my favorite bands as frequently as I could afford. Music, like many of the arts, has the ability to transport you to another place. In this case, it took me right out of the blue.

***

"Animal House," was a hugely popular college frat movie starring John Belushi, which came out in the fall of our senior year. Belushi was a prodigy of "Saturday Night Live," a series of live comedy skits by the SNL players. Intentional or not, John Belushi's raucous and socially displeasing behavior in the movie became something to aspire to for teens looking for a laugh at the expense of their common sense. At Cretin we had one of those high school moments that served as proof that, while we strove to become men, at times, we still had a ways to go.

The cafeteria at Cretin looked like any lunchroom, in any school, anywhere. It was four or five rows of long tables with uncomfortable folding chairs lined up on both sides, serving as a sort of feedlot for teens. The noon hour was staffed by a small contingent of lunch ladies dressed in chef's whites and hairnets. The head of the crew was Mrs. Bean, whose name just happened to be the perfect fit for her career choice. She and her crew prepared food onsite every day. It was the usual fare of an entrée with side accompaniments like soups, potatoes and canned vegetables of various colors. The food was much better than the graffiti in the bathroom stalls alluded to. It was not uncommon to find statements on the wall that read, *Flush twice, it's a long way to the cafeteria.*

I didn't eat hot lunch much. I was a very consistent bag lunch guy. I brought a white bread bologna sandwich, Doritos, and a Little Debbie snack dessert nearly every day of my academic career at Cretin. My friends teased me about my consistency. My idea of variety meant bringing PB&J instead of bologna. I was a creature of habit with boring, white bread sensibilities. My one regular hot lunch splurge though, was getting a big rectangular slice of Mrs. Bean's pizza every Friday. The fact that it was cooked in sheet pans, then sliced and served in big rectangular pieces, led to the references of ingredients on a roofing shingle. To be fair, it was in no way deserving of such a slam. It was delicious.

I sat at lunch with pretty much the same group of friends every day. It was largely the group I went to grade school with at Saint Luke's, namely; Dan, Pat, Pete, and a few other new friends I'd met at Cretin, including Doug. The cafeteria was our halfway through the day decompression chamber from the rigors of our studies. It was where we griped about our English composition due next week, told stories about working at our first jobs, and it served as the think tank for our weekend plans.

In the middle of an average lunch period senior year, a couple of guys suddenly stood up and shouted, "Food fight!" They hurled their sandwiches, apple cores, bags and milk cartons at a table across the lunchroom. Their bologna and cheese assault was not well received. Within seconds, their tosses were countered with fruit, sandwiches and milk containers hurled from the table they had targeted. Soon enough, most of the cafeteria was involved as the fray became a full-on food war.

My friends and I grabbed our lunches and milk and ducked for cover under the table. Half-eaten food, milk cartons and paper lunch bags flew overhead as we crouched down, laughing while we continued eating. None of us wanted to give up our food in the name of adding to the chaos taking place topside. Most of us were rule followers anyway, so while this was amusing, it was certainly nothing we wanted to be associated with.

After a couple minutes the flinging diminished as students, including my friends and I, started heading for the exits. Having had no role in the fracas, we wanted no part in being held to clean the mess up. The event was all the talk in the hallways that afternoon.

To make matters worse, it happened again a couple of days later in a much larger bag lunch brawl. At this point, students were familiar with the drill and evidently more prepared. This time the teaching staff on duty was ready as well. Because of the previous event, the lunch room was monitored and the doors were quickly shut and manned by brothers and teachers. An announcement was made that no students would be allowed to leave until the mess was cleaned up and order restored to the cafeteria. My friends and I were caught in the middle of the uprising, despite our relative innocence. I say relative because one or more of us *may* have chucked something during this encore fray, including me.

Under the now watchful eye of the lunchroom monitors, the students set to picking up the trash and food that was strewn about the place. In a matter of ten minutes the place was back to normal and students were allowed to leave. The cleanup pressure and threat of future sanctions worked, as I don't recall there ever being a third food fight. It's amazing how sometimes all it takes to change teen behavior is a stern warning and making them clean up after themselves.

***

Lunch hours at Cretin were long enough to institute a loosely organized sports program to allow the students to burn off a little youthful energy after we'd finished eating. In the spring, softball was the sport of choice. We were given a couple of aluminum bats and a ball and picked teams among ourselves. Many of the fielders didn't have gloves and played barehanded. In one of these games, I tried to catch a pop up and ended up bending my ring finger in an awkward position. I howled in pain, flapping my hand in agony. My finger swelled up like a Bratwurst and, after a few hours, my class ring began to serve as a finger tourniquet. After school, I ended up at the doctor's office where they cut it off using a tool that looked like a manual can opener. I had it repaired and refit but, within a couple of months, I lost it for good. I have no idea where or how it disappeared, it just did. It was a ring doomed from the start.

In the winter months, we scarfed down our lunches and headed up to the gymnasium for pickup games of "army ball," an ad-hoc mixture of basketball and wrestling. It was played by guys that couldn't make the basketball team, and their play on the court was indicative of why. We typically took off our shoes and our pocket protectors and played in our stocking feet and uniforms. It was a regular occurrence to be driving for a layup only to have one's tie yanked on the way up to the basket. Because there were no rules, these momentary strangulation infractions were completely legal. Army ball was a mixture of horseplay and athletic prowess, but also unregulated, chaotic fun with occasional full-body hockey checks. In the midst of all the military and religious oppression and rules that made up our school environment, it was the lone half hour in our day with almost no rules, so we took full advantage of it. Army ball might have been better termed Anarchy Ball. It was the punk rock of ball sports.

We played hard on the court during these lunch breaks. It was when I first discovered I had a tendency to sweat profusely during workouts. My uniform shirt was usually pitted out by the time the bell rang. I'd gather my belongings up, try and recompose myself and headed to my chemistry class with Mr. Kleinman. After a few days of this, one of the junior students in our class nicknamed me, "Sweatball." Every day when I came in, forehead dripping with sweat, he'd say, "Hey, Sweatball." Luckily it was just a name between the two of us and never caught on with the rest of the class. It's not a redeeming nickname, though, at the time I didn't much care. Army Ball was too much fun not to give it 100%.

CHAPTER 11: COMMUTING

Before my friends and I were old enough to have our drivers' licenses, I undoubtedly had one of the more unusual commutes to a high school on record. I stuck out my thumb and hitchhiked. Hitchhiking was a commonly accepted practice in the seventies and a fair number of Cretin kids did it, so it was my method for getting to school every day. Every morning I walked five blocks to the intersection of Hamline and Summit Avenues. From there, I hitchhiked the last mile or so. Many people picked up Cretin boys because we were assumed to be upstanding citizens, good guys. (Ha! We had them all fooled!) This generation was a simpler time, when hitchhiking didn't mean abduction and sale into the sex traffic trade.

Fortunately for me, there were some regular pickups at the intersection I hitched at. One was Bob Martin's mom in her blue Chevy Impala. She and Bob showed up like clockwork every day twenty minutes before school started. After they picked me up, she picked up every other Cretin kid along the way until we were squeezed in like paratroopers in a jump plane. It got cozy at times, but beggars can't be choosers. More often than not, I was just glad to be out of the weather. Because Mrs. Martin was such a fixture along the route, I made it a point to always try to get there before the appointed time. If I didn't, it meant hoping some other kind soul stopped and delivered me to my destination. It also taught me that with any free ride, you never knew what kind of driver you were going to dial up.

If I managed to miss my ride with the Martins, one of my fallbacks was a guy who picked me up in his Volkswagen Beetle. The front seat was cramped and the interior simplistic and utilitarian. This minimalist, clown car didn't even have a dashboard. Each time I climbed in, the windshield seemed no more than twelve inches from my face. The defroster was a series of small vents at the base of the nearly vertical windshield. During our winter rides, heat was nothing more than a false promise from an engineering team pissed off about the results of World War II. It wasn't happening.

From a performance standpoint, the four speed shifter on the floor was toy-like and the sewing machine engine was built for people with low expectations. And, while the guy was nice enough and his intentions noble, his transportation was stripped down and basic. When you're hitchhiking, any vehicle with four wheels and a roof is good enough. A ride in this guy's bug was a step up from a bike and a step down from taking the bus.

Perhaps the strangest ride I ever took to school came sophomore year. One morning a couple of upperclassmen from my school picked me up in their Ford beater. I knew one of the guys. He lived near us and ran with the party crowd but, because I was a straight-kid, our paths didn't cross much. When I jumped into the back seat, I was overcome by the smell of weed. The stereo was blasting Led Zeppelin and it seemed the boys in the front seat were doing a little "wake 'n' bake." It was odd to see a couple of guys in military uniforms toking up at 7:30 in the morning. High school meant different things to different people, I guess. I was a little mortified by the whole situation I'd stepped into.

How can people live this way? What if we get stopped? What if someone smells it on me at school? I wonder if reform school has a soccer team?

I was such a self-righteous, innocent geek.

"Hey, man, want a hit?" the passenger asked, passing the joint over the front seat.

"Nah, I'm good. Thanks, though."

I had yet to try pot, and thought, when I do, first thing in the morning on the way to school might not be the best time to experiment.

The guys were cool about it and just shrugged it off. We made it to school okay, and the stoners were nice enough to drop me at the front door before they parked in the lot and, I'm guessing, finished the doobie. After I got out, in my insecurity, I thought maybe I should have imbibed, if for nothing else than just to be accepted as one of the cool kids. At that age, nothing was more important than being accepted, even if it was by the burn outs. Looking back, I'm glad I was confident or, maybe afraid enough, to resist the temptation. I had to work hard enough in school to maintain a B average. The last thing I needed was to try a drug that makes you inattentive and stupid while under its influence. Geometry was hard enough for me stone sober.

***

Hitchhiking home from school was a slightly different scenario. Because Hamline Avenue, my main route home, was often crowded with other hitchhikers, a few friends and I took the Randolph bus east to Lexington Avenue and hitched from there. We had a regular pickup on that route. It was a large black woman who drove a dually, a heavy duty pickup with four wheels in the back instead of two. We always wondered why she needed such a big truck, but were never brave enough to ask. She was a pleasant but quiet woman, who took each of us to our appointed corners and dropped us off. After a while she even knew who got off where. We never got her name, but between ourselves we gave her the name, Big Mama. She was a large woman in a big truck who treated us like family, so the name just kind of stuck. Frankly, anyone kind enough to pick us up sort of became like family, even if just for a few minutes during our commute.

At the time, hitchhiking seemed like such an innocuous thing. My brother had done it when he went to Cretin and my friends did it all the time, so I never gave it a second thought. When I tell people today about it, I usually get a look of disbelief. But, in a single parent family with six children and one car, you are forced to make accommodations and getting to school was one of them. I sometimes wish our world was more like the world of those days. What better way to meet people than to travel with them for a short time from A to B? It brought a few characters into my own life experience, made it a little richer and saved a little gasoline in the process.

***

During the late seventies the country was still recovering from its first real oil crisis. Oil embargoes instituted by Arab countries had driven prices high and in some cases made shortages a day-to-day reality. People started seeking alternative, more efficient transportation vehicles and methods to cut corners on gas consumption and save money.

My buddy Pete's parents somehow came across one of these forms that never really caught on. It was called a Pedicar. It was a two seat, four wheeled, open-aired vehicle with a little room for storage in the back. In some ways, it resembled a hot tub on wheels. The cockpit of the thing had a stick shift in the middle that moved the chain among the various sprockets and gears for assistance with hills. Both the driver and the passenger had pedals, so the load was shared between them. There was a hand brake as well. Sometimes it even worked. But, sometimes not.

As teenagers who all lived within a few blocks of one another, Pete, Pat and I were a rat pack that travelled everywhere in threes. We were inseparable. So, when Pete showed us the crudely made vehicle, our curiosity got the better of us. By this time we all had our licenses to drive an ordinary car, but the thought of a ride in this oversized fiberglass clamshell on wheels was too good to pass up. We had to try it out. Because it was made for two, we determined we would be remiss if we didn't push it to its structural carrying capacity by overloading it with a third person. To deny one of us access to the fun that the other two were destined to encounter was unthinkable. Besides, what could possibly go wrong?

A little before dusk one summer evening, we piled into what looked like a four-wheeled Jacuzzi. Pat and Pete took the pilot/copilot seats while I was relegated to the would-be trunk.

"Here we go, boys! Where should we go?" Pete asked.

"Let's take a run down to Grand Avenue," I answered.

"Sounds good!"

Pat and Pete strained to get the pedals started. The vehicle was geared low, but the weight of the third passenger made starting laborious. The spoke wheels turned slowly as the two of them cranked the pedals and started gaining momentum. When we hit the small downward incline on Pete's driveway we started picking up speed entering into Summit Avenue. Pete braked and signaled a right turn with his left arm out the side of the Pedicar as we all craned our heads left hoping there were no cars coming in the lane we were entering. Without regard for a full stop, we coasted into Summit Avenue.

Pete completed the turn and we rode in the lane closest to the curb. We occupied it like a big, fat annoying bike without the height advantage to make us visible in rear view mirrors. In essence, we were now travelling in a roadway with no visible illumination, at dusk, invisible to most blind spots and with no seat belts, helmets or common sense. We were multiple offenders on the move.

The vehicle handled like the rolling hot tub it was. It was slow, for one thing. There was certainly no way we were ever going to get a speeding ticket, that much was sure. Impeding traffic maybe, but not speeding. We were completely free though, not exactly kings of the road, but surely princes. As cars passed us, motorists gawked out their windows or honked in annoyance. In some strange way, it was exhilarating moving about in something outside the realm of just another boring car. It was juvenile recklessness and it was life-giving.

At the same time, it wasn't difficult to speculate on the thoughts in the heads of the people around us.

"Hey, look at those stupid kids in that stupid thing! What is that dang thing?"

We chugged on down Summit Avenue until we came to the intersection of Oxford where Pete steered the vehicle into the left lane and put his arm out signaling a left turn. Somehow, being in a left turn lane made our exposure and vulnerability a lot more apparent. We were IN TRAFFIC, MAN! Cars whizzed by in the opposite direction as we got a new appreciation for how fast thirty miles an hour really was.

We made a slow left onto Oxford, a side street with a slight downhill, so gravity had its way and we began building speed. The nervous laughter started as we hurtled toward Grand Avenue, a much busier thoroughfare than Oxford or Summit. The odds we would come to a traffic-free intersection were much smaller. It was a roll of the dice we hadn't given much thought to when I recommended it.

"Hey! You might want to shift to a lower gear to slow us down, Pete," I screamed from the rumble seat.

Pete pulled on the gear stick and nothing happened. He said with a mixture of laughter and alarm, "We have no gears!"

"Well, hit the brakes, man!" Pat said.

Pete squeezed the brakes and while the vehicle slowed slightly it was not enough to lend a sense of safety to any of us.

"Um, we have no brakes, either!"

"What do you mean we have no brakes?" I asked.

"We have no brakes!" Pete screeched.

The Pedicar suddenly filled with an uneasy laughter from its helpless passengers. We were a rolling liability.

"We're all gonna die!" I said trying to lighten the mood before our impending disaster.

"Hold on," Pete said, gripping the wheel with focus and intent. Pat and I weren't sure whether Pete was overstating the magnitude of our malfunctions to scare us, but one thing was sure, we were at the mercy of our own James Lovell on this, our Apollo 13.

Pete swiveled his head from left to right to see if any cars were approaching from the lane we were ultimately going to have to turn into. He gripped the steering wheel tightly. It seemed it was his only working instrument on the whole vehicle. I signaled a right turn from the trunk area, in case there were cars coming, as if a signal would help. It was my desperate way of helping divert us from a yet unverified but seemingly inevitable collision. We hurtled forward, all three of us leaning to the right as we began our ninety degree right turn. The car shook with resistance, a reminder we were taxing not only its weight limit, but its cornering agility. All of it conducted at a speed never intended for the engineering hold-my-beer prototype we were now at the mercy of.

By either God's grace or the post-dinner traffic pattern slowdown, we careened through the corner without encountering an oncoming car. Pete again quickly steered us into the lane nearest the curb. He and Pat resumed pedaling, trying to look nonchalant about the bullet we'd just dodged. Nothing to see here, folks. Just a brush with death for three teens. Carry on.

"Whooee!" Pete hollered. "That was close."

"Yeah, let's not do that again," Pat added.

We laughed and recounted the anxious moment amongst one another. Pete steered the vehicle down Grand Avenue, pumping his legs alongside Pat as we began working ourselves back toward Pete's house. It seems our stress test on the Pedicar revealed it was unsafe at any speed, at least under the guidance of Larry, Mo and Curly, as it were. It was a Corvair with pedals.

After another fifteen minutes of pedaling and a handful of car honks, waves and a couple of single digit salutes directed our way, we arrived back at Pete's house. Our maiden, and ultimately, only voyage in the vehicle had gone about as badly as it could have. On the upside, we didn't roll it over, not for lack of trying. It was clear this energy saving mode of transport was not quite ready for prime time. Or, maybe it just required an older, more responsible crew at the controls. Whatever the case, it was fun while it lasted and it beat the pants off an otherwise boring trip in a real car.

CHAPTER 12: TEACHERS

When it came to teachers, Len Horyza was one of the good guys. He taught sophomore geometry and upper level trigonometry. Clean shaven and sporting his trademark crew cut, he was also coach of the varsity basketball team. The appeal in his teaching methods was his laid back nature. His classes were light and fun. He had a wicked sense of humor and used it with regularity in the classroom. At the same time, if someone pushed the limits of order, he was quick to issue a military punishment befitting the infraction…push-ups. His standard line was the "drop and give me twenty." He always followed up this directive with, "I want to hear your belt buckle hit the ground with each one. And, no honeymoon push-ups, either." We quickly learned a honeymoon pushup was when you didn't keep your back straight and looked a little bit like, well, like you were on your honeymoon. And I don't mean the staring at Niagara Falls part, either.

Mr. Horyza was a masterful teacher. I was never a fan of math nor very good at it, but he made geometry understandable and fun. We often worked through geometry problems as a class. Each of the word problems involved a series of steps to get to the solution. Keys to the solution were unearthed by finding a radius or hypotenuse, using sine, cosine and other long forgotten means. Every once in a while one of the steps was to say that an answer was "given," meaning it was provided in the description somewhere as a known figure. Sometimes when students didn't have a clue what answer Mr. Horyza was looking for they answered him with "uh, given?" He usually mocked those students. "Given! That's the standard for, I dunno. You realize that, right?" he'd ask. The response was usually a guilty grin from the student. Horyza was good at calling peoples' bluffs.

One of the requirements for geometry class was keeping a notebook with homework assignments in it. These notebooks weren't really checked until the end of the quarter, so you could get away with slacking, if you wanted. My friend Dan, near the end of every quarter approached me and said, "So, you gonna lend me your notebook so I can copy it tonight?"

"Dude, you know it's cheating, right?"

"Oh, no, I have all the homework done. It's just yours is so much neater and I need to check my work and stuff."

"Hmmm… I don't know…it might cost ya."

"C'mon, Landwehr. I'll buy you a shake at lunch tomorrow," he pleaded.

Now, I don't condone cheating, except in the name of free enterprise, maybe. Add to it that this was a good friend, and I guess I might have loaned my notebook to him once or twice. I think. Maybe, yeah. In his defense, I knew he'd done the homework and was just looking to improve the readability.

To show how much it really matters, he went on to be a successful attorney with no evident need for a good grasp of Pythagoras' Theorem or a pristine notebook to show for it. I think I can grant a little mercy.

***

Perhaps my favorite teacher in my four years of high school was Mr. Tierney. He taught current events and social studies and his style was completely outside the box. His methods led to the nickname, Wild Bill for his ability to rile students up in the name of justice and social consciousness. His lessons encouraged us to think for ourselves and see past the veneer of popular culture. He challenged us to research issues of social equality and consumer rights that raised our ire. He knew young voices were the ones that could change the world and was doing his part to energize us.

Like Len Horyza and his "drop and give me twenty," Mr. Tierney had his own quote that became his tag line. "It's the corporations!" he'd shout. He linked most of America's woes to corporate greed and capitalism.

"They don't care about you, or the environment! All the corporations care about is the almighty dollar. Are you going to sit by and let them control your mind and your spending without questioning their motives?" he'd ask, his voice hitting a fevered pitch. As young people, many of us were plodding along in the complacent and compliant footsteps of our parents and our government. Mr. Tierney taught us to think for ourselves, to question authority and to confront injustices head on.

At the time, Tom Ogle, an American inventor, had come out with the claim of a carburetor system that would enable a normal car to get up to one hundred miles on a gallon of gas. While Mr. Tierney was excited at the promise of such an innovation, he also said the invention will probably never see the light of day.

"Big oil is going to come in and buy him out and make sure this project goes away. Because corporations don't care about doing what's right! Especially if it doesn't benefit them the way they want."

It turns out he was right. Ogle's invention never came to be and Tom Ogle died mysteriously in 1981 of an overdose of Darvon and alcohol. Some say it was no accident, rather he was actually poisoned. Mr. Tierney had pegged corporate America for the scoundrels they really were.

Sometimes a whole class was spent on a single environmental or political event. Lectures ambled and moseyed along like a stream of consciousness. If any individual felt strongly about a topic, Mr. Tierney would encourage that person to bring a presentation about it to the class. If they weren't keen on a formal presentation, he gave them free reign to write their findings or thoughts on the blackboard for the whole class to see. Then, he'd sometimes leave them there for days. It was an attempt to push our conventions, to free-think and to empower the proletariat. His thinking and style were so far outside the oppressiveness and conformity imposed on us by our religion and military classes. I found his spin on teaching positively liberating. For a man our fathers' age, he was cool! A short-haired hippy disguised by his shirt and tie.

I was always a little curious what the other, more conventional teachers at Cretin thought of his technique. There's little doubt he got us riled up from class to class, depending on the subject. During one class he pointed out that we should be upset at the radiation we were being pummeled with by the fluorescent lights overhead.

"Who knows what these fluorescent rays are doing to us? They may be making us stupid. Maybe even brain cancer! We don't know and we shouldn't just live with it! It's the corporations!"

I looked up and began to wonder if he wasn't on to something. It was the start of questioning a lot of things for my young mind.

On another occasion Mr. Tierney quoted some of Bob Dylan's lyrics for "All Along the Watchtower," and asked if anyone knew where the quote came from. When Pat Hewitt answered correctly, Mr. Tierney had him write the lyrics on the board. I'm not sure of the context that dredged up the topic in the first place, but I thought it was pretty cool to have rock lyrics on the board instead of some dry socio-cultural fact or reading assignment. You just didn't see Dylan on the blackboard every day. It's those kinds of things that were the reason he was voted favorite faculty member in the yearbook poll.

Part of what made Mr. Tierney so cool was he taught us but never talked down to students, encouraging us to think like the young adults we were. We Cretin boys were the future of America, and he saw the potential in that. In my mind Mr. Tierney was ahead of his time. The closest parallel I can think of is Robin Williams and his teaching practices in the movie, *Dead Poets Society*. And while Mr. Tierney never encouraged us to stand on our desks to get a fresh perspective, I am certain he would have approved if we did.

***

Much of the Cretin staff was made up of Christian Brothers. These were men committed to the Christian faith, who lived on-site in a residence attached to the school. The oldest of these brothers during my years was Brother Pius. He was about a hundred and ten years old when I started – at least it seemed that way. He was a frail wisp of a man, and at his advanced age had lost much of his hearing. By the time my class arrived as freshmen, his teaching days were over and he was pretty much in charge of one task - cafeteria lunch line duty.

At noon a line formed outside the cafeteria every day, and Brother Pius was the holy gatekeeper. He was the bridge troll between us and a hot lunch. Brother sat in his chair at the doorway to the lunch counter and served to control the crush inside the service area. His walking cane doubled as a lift gate entrance into the buffet line. When it was held between him and the door, you stayed where you were. When he let it down, you were welcome to go in. Sitting like a lunch cop in his long black brothers' garments and white collar, toothpick in his teeth, he picked away and regulated the traffic flow. He was a harmless, loveable guy who'd served his time as a teacher and had been relegated to the pasture fields of the cafeteria, a job he took very seriously.

One day on his birthday, my friend Pat went up to him and said loudly, "Happy birthday, Brother."

Brother Pius replied, "Thank you, thank you."

Trying to continue the conversation, Pat said, "So how old are you today, Brother?"

"Thank you, thank you," responded Brother, as he dropped the cane and let Pat through.

So much for extending that dialogue.

Because Brother Pius was so old and frail for so many years he acquired the moniker Brother Free Day. The thinking was, he was such a stalwart fixture around Cretin for so long that when he died, school would certainly be cancelled to honor his legacy. I cannot deny the twisted thinking behind this cruel nickname, but these were high school boys we are talking about. The funny thing was that my older brother, whose class graduated six years prior, referred to him with the same name, and they held the same expectation. Certainly no student over the years wished him ill will, but no one thought he'd outlive their high school tenure either. He was a resilient one.

After I left Cretin, I lost track of whatever happened to Brother Pius. I did hear that when he died, there was no day off for *anyone*. I'm fairly sure it was a statement made by the administration because they'd heard the nickname over the years and purposely didn't grant a day off just for reasons of spite. And I guess that puts a fairly mean title in its rightful place.

***

Like any school, not all of the staff at Cretin were student favorites. I suspect everyone has a story or two about a high school teacher who was either biding their time or whose teaching style left something to be desired. For myself, one of those was my freshman algebra teacher, Harvey Buron. I realize I may be alienating some who knew and loved him, as he was sort of an icon around the school. He was coach of the varsity soccer team and the celebrated hero of the annual fundraising SPAFF festival, that dreaded fundraiser I loathed in so many ways. It seemed he taught at Cretin from the beginning of World War I, and to me was clearly one of those that should have quit teaching years earlier when he lost interest in it. I suspect we all had teachers like that in our pasts.

From the desk of a student, Harvey came across as a cantankerous, crotchety old man. He was heavyset, bald, and walked with a slow lumbering gait. His tone was always a gruff state of crabby, and he rarely smiled. If you answered a question incorrectly, you were sometimes dealt a handful of pity or ridicule. And he had a death stare that could turn you into a pillar of salt if he caught you goofing off. I guess these traits probably develop when you spend a long time working with teenage students, as Harvey did. At the same time, I thought if you're not happy with what you're doing, do something else and make room for a teacher that doesn't appear at the end of his rope from day to day.

Nothing epitomized the teaching style of Mr. Buron as much as one of his instructional aids, or so I'll call it. At his desk he had a thin walking cane which he loosely threatened to use on students who acted up. The first day of freshman algebra class, he said, "I have a good friend for those of you who like to push boundaries." He lifted the cane before the class and said, "I call this Polyastre. Now for those of you who don't know, poly means many, and astre is the technical term for stars. Put it together and I think you get the picture. Many stars." He then went on to explain that the tape on the cane was to repair it after an incident, shall we call it.

Now, I get the whole old school discipline thing. After all, I grew up within the Catholic school system. But this was the first day of freshman year in a new school. I am sure Mr. Buron was just establishing his dominance and laying the ground rules for law and order. But as his introduction to a new crop of adolescent boys, I thought it was a bit over the top of the old guy. His persona resonated with the angry schoolmaster Pink Floyd lyric of *Another Brick in the Wall*, "If you don't eat your meat, ya can't have any pudding!"

I don't believe Harvey ever caned anyone during my four years at Cretin, so maybe it was a good incentive to good behavior. But I sometimes wonder what kind of backlash a reference to a punitive measure that causes "many stars" might have if it were uttered in a classroom today. I realize it was a different time back then, but still. I also think it's worth noting that the teachers who resonate as some of my favorites were some of the more sensitive and funny ones. The heavy-handed dictatorial types always fell to the bottom of the list for me. I am pretty sure his disdain for me was mutual. There were guys that thought he was great, and maybe he was. He just wasn't my favorite, and I think everyone's entitled to that.

***

There were a few other teachers whose idiosyncrasies made them, well let's just say, unique. One was Brother Lionel, a big fella with the hulk of a professional boxer. He was our physical education teacher and he suffered from a terrible stutter. I always felt extremely bad for him. One of his famous tactics when he got riled by a student was to get in their face and say "What are yyyyyou a Saint Paul t-t-tough guy or sumpin?" Despite being a gentle giant in most situations, when he was ticked off his big, imposing presence struck fear into the hearts of those who crossed him.

One of the requirements of gym was we had to wear jock straps as part of our physical education uniforms. Because some kids were self-conscious about being naked in the locker room while changing, they just wore their briefs underneath their shorts. For the most part these "tighty whities," were more than enough support. Brother Lionel was a stickler for details, though and was not afraid to ask boys if they were really wearing a jock or not. A little weird? Um, yes. A bit invasive? Yeah, highly.

I don't want to paint Brother Lionel as a pervert or anything. It was a different time, and I am certain he was only looking out for our safety – didn't want anyone getting a hernia or anything. In actual fact, Brother had a huge heart and a soft side to him. If he sensed a kid had something going on in his life he would take him aside and talk to him about it. He genuinely cared and would give kids words of advice when they probably needed them most. His good attributes fostered in him by the Christian brotherhood were *very* good.

His soft side came to the surface one day when we were outside on the running track. He said he sensed that as freshmen, we were between an age of boy and man. He said he wanted us to relive our innocence by going back to our youth and playing in the long jump sand pit as though we were kids playing in the sandbox. His claim was that as teenagers, we probably never got a chance to go back and play like we were kids.

"Get, in tttttouch with your inner ch-child," he said.

We all kind of stood around looking awkwardly at one another. One after another we sat in the pit and started faux playing in the sand. Frankly, as teens, the very thing he was trying to get us in touch with was what we were seeking to put behind us. We just wanted to run the low hurdles, or whatever. The whole event seemed as weird as it sounds, but I get what he was trying to do. His intentions were good, just a tad unorthodox.

***

Brother Martell got a bad rap. Going into my freshman year, my brother Tom warned me how tough he was. I'd heard the same from other friends whose brothers had come through the system at Cretin. My first real exposure to him was actually the summer before I started. Because it was a private school and tuition expensive, our family qualified for student work study. This meant spending a few weeks of summer mornings at school doing grunt work at a low wage which would be applied directly to student tuition. Mom needed all the financial help she could get, so we took advantage of any opportunities afforded us.

Brother Martell was the chief overseer of me and a couple of other lackeys charged with getting the school and grounds in shape for the '75/'76 school year. Brother was stocky, sported a crew cut and carried himself with confidence. His stature was in direct contrast to his lisp that made him sound a little like Elmer Fudd. Behind his back, students referred to him as Bwudda Mowtelw. It was hard for me not to make the Fudd correlation, but over time we all got used to it and his speech became more a quality of endearment.

On my first day of work study, he greeted me and informed me that we would be "mowing gwass." He set me up with a push mower and showed me the basics on gas, oil and spark. Then he emphasized how important it was to scrape the large grass chunks off the bottom of the mower deck using a putty knife. It made the mower lighter and easier to move and made the engine work more efficiently. I mowed for most of the morning with Brother making occasional check-ins to see how I was doing.

As the summer wore on, we moved indoors to clean desks using an industrial cleaner/disinfectant that, judging from its smell, there were reasons it was not sold for home use. I'm sure it did its part to decay the ozone layer, to say nothing of my young lungs. Another indoor task involved scraping off the dried up chewing gum from the bottom of the desks. This was required from year to year, and it certainly gave me a new appreciation for not chewing gum in class.

A few years later, I had Brother Martell as my religion teacher. I heard he was a tough, but fair grader. He was a stickler for the rules and laws of school order, and Lord help the student that didn't have an out-of-uniform permit while out of uniform in his class. Rumors also circulated Brother had some sort of police authority. He was either trained as an undercover officer or had some arresting authority with a focus on narcotics. The rumor was enough to keep most of us on the straight and narrow. I wasn't much of a rule breaker anyways, at least not within school walls.

Brother had a unique teaching method using ornate chalkboard artwork and lesson planning. It was engaging and eye catching. He taught from the Book of Acts and others in our school-issued black Catholic Bibles. The way he tied all of it into the importance of salvation and our redemption from sin was effective and lasting. He emphasized the separation of man from God and relayed it to us, the next generation, with meaning and purpose. One phrase he used frequently was, "The white worms are waiting for you, gentlemen," referring to our ultimate fate as worm food when we're dead and gone. It was nothing if not a wakeup call to live our lives with immediacy and intentionality. It was his greatest gift to me.

***

There were a multitude of other memorable teachers at Cretin over the years. One of them was my freshman religion and human development teacher, Brother Gerard. He was a frail, senior Brother who was tasked with teaching us Biblical truth while at the same time discussing human sexual anatomy and addressing embarrassing subjects like masturbation, intercourse and birth control. It seemed strange to mix the message of "don't do this" with, "but if you do this other thing, then do this." It was even weirder because it was coming from someone apparently older than my grandparents, from a man who had pledged himself to a life of celibacy and to abstaining from all of it. To me, it was a little like putting a nun in charge of a brothel. Good luck!

One of the practices of the religion portion of Brother Gerard's curriculum was requiring students keep a notebook with some of his relevant high points during lecture. I was uncertain about what he wanted or, perhaps disinterested, so mine was not what one would deem the most stellar among the class. Some students put great effort into their work. Because I was busy trying to get through harder classes like algebra and biology, religion and its related homework took a back seat. How hard could it be to understand the Gospel message of Christ coming to save us from our sins? I fully understood it and it seemed like Christ would afford me a little grace for a neglected notebook.

Right before our winter break, we were required to hand them in. Brother went through and graded them. When it came time to hand them back, he called me out in front of the whole class saying, "Mr. Landwehr, I'm disappointed in your notebook and am sending a blue slip home to your parents."

Hold up! Stop the train! A BLUE slip? A blue slip was a nastygram notification to your parents, a heads up that their child was at a D grade level. It was common knowledge that only crappy students got blue slips sent home, and I was certainly not a crappy student. In my mind I rationalized the bad grade by attributing it to Brother Gerard being a lousy teacher – one of those I thought should have been given the hook a few years earlier. In reality, it was probably a little of both. I was no model student, but his methods were less than engaging as well.

Over Christmas break, Mom got the blue slip in the mail, and I had to song and dance my way out of it. "Mom, he didn't like my notebook. I don't think he likes me either, and frankly, the feeling is mutual. I'll get my grade back up after break. It's no big deal," I said in my defense. Mom knew I sometimes struggled in school and usually cut me slack, because in the end, she knew I'd come out squarely in the middle with a B average. I was a solid B student, something Mom strongly encouraged, because it qualified us for the good student discount on our auto insurance. I got my share of C's for sure, but I consistently managed to average them out with an A in something else.

Getting that blue slip was probably the biggest slap in the face and wakeup call of my entire academic career. I obsessed and worried about it my entire Christmas vacation. I also have to confess, I thought some pretty hateful thoughts as well. I knew Brother Gerard was in bad health going into the break. He'd had much of his stomach removed as part of some sort of cancer and occasionally had to excuse himself from class to deal with digestion issues. It was kind of sad he still had to teach at all, given his health.

While I felt bad Brother was in such poor health, I couldn't help but wish for some misfortune to befall him over Christmas break. I didn't wish him dead, but rather I hoped his failing health would prohibit him from returning to teach after Christmas. It would be the best Christmas gift I could get, at least through the eyes of an academically struggling religion student.

Well, imagine my surprise when I returned to school to find out Brother Gerard had passed away over Christmas break and would be replaced by another lay teacher. *He what? He died? What the heck?* It appeared as though my thought life had gone and killed a man.

I never meant to kill the guy. Really, I didn't.

As if all the Catholic guilt for every other sin I'd committed and carried with me up to this point wasn't enough. Now I had to deal with a lifetime of guilt for my manslaughter charge. All because of a stupid blue slip!

To confess even further, once I was over the initial guilt and shock of Brother's passing, I had to publicly quell my relief and excitement at being handed this new opportunity. I looked at it as my chance at academic redemption and promised I would work to never get a blue slip sent home again. I recognize it was a twisted thought at the time, and continues to be for that matter, but it at least spurred me to push myself and get my head back into my schoolwork.

They filled his vacant position with Mr. Riley, a young, hip lay teacher. He taught the sex education portion of class from a position of someone who had at least been there, and presented the materials in a frank and more relatable manner. His methods made the class engaging and, with a little more focus, I was able to pass the class with a B minus. In part to justify my guilt, I credit my grade to Brother Gerard's teaching legacy. His disciplinary note did the trick, even in the presence of his absence.

***

I suspect it is like this in most schools, but there were some teachers at Cretin that were not very good at managing a classroom. As students, we sniffed out the weak and made their teaching lives incredibly difficult. I know if I were charged with keeping twenty-five teenage boys under control and interested in a topic, I would likely be in a federal penitentiary today. I know myself.

Mr. Gaertner was one of the weak. A short, geeky looking fellow with greasy hair and nerdy glasses right out of the '50s, he taught Spanish to everyone but freshman. He wore a shirt and tie and suitcoat to work every day. And, I mean literally, the same suit coat, every day. It was blue and gray and had done hard time at Cretin over the years. I understand clothing is expensive, especially suits, but maybe dial up a three coat rotation to keep us guessing.

Mr. Gaertner's facial features gave him a rodent like appearance. For years he was known at Cretin as Mouse. Teenage boys can be horrible humans, so this labeling of a teacher by students seemed perfectly normal. He looked like a mouse, so we called him Mouse. To make him even more a target, he had a wandering eye, so you were never quite sure if he was looking at you or the guy next to you. Again, teens fixate on these sorts of things, so Mouse never had a chance.

Occasionally during class kids wandering the halls shouted, "Mouse!" at the top of their lungs. Other times, they slammed his door shut and took off running. The slam always sounded like a gunshot, taking us all by surprise. Sometimes, there was even the double combo of "Mouse!" Slam! How these disruptors were able to roam the halls during class time, I have no idea. It was a different time.

Despite his poor classroom management skills, he was a pretty decent teacher. He had a method to his madness for memorizing the language. One thing that was hammered home was a practical way to memorize the six various verb endings. He'd rattle them off, "i, iste, io, imos, isteis." The sixth one was, "ieron" for which he always said, "And our old favorite, i, e, Ron… Johnson." He always hung his words at the Ron part, waiting for the class to chime in with Johnson.

Ron Johnson was a famous football player to only Mr. Gaertner, evidently. None of us knew who he was. He liked throwing Johnson's name as a memory tag. It worked, obviously, but none of us knew who we was talking about, so the joke was lost on us. He certainly enjoyed replaying the reference every time he recited the verb endings though. Over time, some of the wise guys in the class got funny with him and instead of answering with Johnson they answered with Jackson or McDonald.

As I said though, Mouse was a good educator. He was fair and had a policy that anyone who did poorly but re-took an exam or quiz of his would never be graded lower than a C for the retake. I will admit this saved me more than once. In addition to the fact that he was a decent teacher, I always felt a little bad for Mr. Gaertner. He didn't deserve what we students put him through. Teachers in general deserve better than what they have to put up with during their teaching years, that much is sure. If we'd only known then what we know as adults, we might have been kinder during our high school years.

***

There were a few teachers at Cretin you just didn't cross. Every school has them, I suppose. The tough guys. Guys that have taken grief for a few years too many and are fed up with it. Or, guys with chips on their shoulders for some reason and maybe just looking for a little backlash to set off their wrath. It was a different time in the late '70s than it is today, a time when teachers could take matters, and, in some cases, students, into their own hands in the name of discipline.

And I don't necessarily begrudge those guys for what they did. Teenage boys can be smart-mouthed jerks and, frankly, sometimes we deserved what we got. Not always, but there were moments. I don't mean to liken the teachers to prison guards, but after all, it was an all-male setting and, at times, tempers rose.

Our English teacher, Brother Blaise, was one of the guys not afraid to take a kid out to the hall, grab him by the collar and push him up against the lockers. I'd heard it done at least once, as the story rippled through the school. Things like that don't go unnoticed from student to student. It is likely the kid said something worthy of the stern warning, but you just don't see things like that happening these days, at least not without some sort of corrective action.

Brother had lots of good qualities too, though. He was a pretty good English teacher and admittedly somewhat of an inspiration for my own love of English, writing and public speaking. He did have a unique speech pattern however. When calling on students, he slipped in an "ah" between the first and last name, or at least he did consistently with mine. Always quick to pick up on things like that, my friends quickly dubbed me James Ah Landwehr. After a time, it turned into just, James Ah.

Another of the tough guys was Brother Kevin. As Dean of Discipline, he actually had it in his title to be able to take matters into his own hands. In his 30s, Brother Kevin had a full beard, steely eyes and a get-it-done attitude, particularly when it came to drug checks. He took his authority to new levels by cutting locks off lockers suspected of containing drugs. Brother never seemed to need more than a sneaking suspicion to wield his bolt cutters and start snipping away. It didn't make him a highly popular guy around school, especially for those who fell victim to his locker entry. But he wasn't the kind of Christian Brother who made it a goal to be best buds with the students anyway. His goal was a drug-free righteousness, by whatever means necessary. I'm certain he had other duties as Dean of Discipline, but for me, and likely many of my classmates, he was the drug-sniffing czar of the administration.

Of course there were Christian Brothers that could shame you with their words. Brother Jaime, our Freshman Spanish teacher made a point of telling guys not to be "estupido" when he felt they needed a reminder. It was meant harmlessly, and often taken as such, but something you don't often hear teachers calling students these days. Or, if a student gave a lame reason why they did not have their homework done, he belittled them by saying, "Oh, pobrecito, wah, wah, wah." Again, it was harmless, but a phrase that let you know your place.

For every one of the hard nose or insensitive teachers, there was one that was too passive or docile. Another Brother Gerard (aka, the "other Brother Gerard") was one of these soft-hearted souls who tended to get walked on for his kindness. Instead of taking guys on with brute force or stern looks, he'd defer to his trademark phrase, "That's grammar school, Mister." If the nonsense persisted, it became just, "grammar school," and we could fill in the rest. It was a saying we picked up as friends and used on one another when we were annoyed. "Grammar school, Pete," and so on. It was our backhanded way of picking on the teachers we actually liked because they seemed to have a compassionate, soft side that some of the other teachers did not.

Looking back, we had it pretty good with the teachers and staff of Cretin. Every school then and now has its model teachers as well as the clunkers. In the end, I came away with a B average and a leg up for moving on to college, so I can't complain. For the most part, they were fair and genuinely cared about educating us as best they could. Some days it was more like "Lord of the Flies" or "Animal House" than an institution of higher learning. So kudos go out to those that made order out of the chaos and trained us as young men to go into the world a little smarter, and as better human beings.

CHAPTER 13: SPORTS

I had a short, lackluster athletic career at Cretin, starting my freshman year when I tried out for the football team. I loved playing football in middle school and was coming off a year of warming the bench for the eighth grade team at Saint Luke's. That team won the Twin Cities parochial championship a year earlier and our success had pumped me up to play in high school, despite the prospect of warming the bench again. I was a small kid with realistic expectations of my abilities, but like I said, I absolutely loved the sport. Guys like me and Dan Nayman stood barely over 5 feet and hardly a granola bar over a hundred pounds, but we wanted to play so bad we were willing to tough it out.

On a weekday in July of 1975, we were to report for team orientation, equipment fitting and issue. As I walked in the door, the hallways were dimly lit and silent except for the echoes of my footfalls. The start of school was still a few weeks away and I knew that soon enough, these halls would be filled with the adolescent energy of uniformed students carrying books to chemistry, English and algebra. At the moment however, as I walked beneath the large framed class photos of those who had gone before me, it was a lonely place for me, a stranger to these halls. I passed through the main building and crossed the driveway to the annex.

After a meeting in the annex where we filled out paperwork and were oriented by the staff, we were herded back to the main building, then downstairs to the locker rooms. We milled around awaiting direction from Brother Walter and the coaches, Mr. Kleinman and Mr. Youngdall. Brother Walter was a tall, barrel chested guy in his thirties. He had an upbeat, pleasant demeanor and always seemed to wear a smile. He was dressed in black trousers, black shirt with a white collar, the casual uniform of the clergy. Brother had a distracting shoulder twitch, where every minute or so he would roll a shoulder or adjust his shirt with a tug. I'm unsure whether it was a nervous twitch thing or a manifestation of Tourette's syndrome. After a while, I got used to it and barely noticed it.

Once our mob was assembled, we were split off into groups based on what position we hoped to play. I was a little shocked at the size of the guys on the team. I was not only one of the shortest guys, but it looked like I was one of the lightest too. At a little over a hundred pounds it appeared I was a boy among giants. A few of the guys even had significant facial hair – something I could only dream about from where I was at. I really wanted to play though, so all of these intimidating variables would have to take a back seat to me giving it my best and seeing how things shook out. I took my place in line among the wide receivers thinking it was a good fit given my size. Catch the ball, score a touchdown, be a hero. It seemed pretty simple.

After sign-in and roll call, we were given instructions on how the equipment distribution would work. Next, we were weighed and measured for our height. From there, we shuffled from station to station for the equipment fitting. We moved from pants and their associated pads, to helmets and then to shoulder pads. At the shoulder pad station, I was sized up and handed a pair to try on. They were well worn and the mesh covered foam reeked of the sweat-laden two-a-day practices of adolescent boys from previous years. The smell was positively sinus clearing. When I found a pair that were deemed good enough, I was sent on my way to the equipment purchase counter to buy my other incidentals like a mouth guard, jockstrap and cup.

I had never worn a jock or cup in middle school. I was a fairly self-conscious kid, so the thought of changing into something as exposing as a jock strap – in front of people, nonetheless – seemed about as threatening as you could get. So, in middle school for all games and practices, tighty-whities it was. A thin layer of bleached cotton was all that stood between injury and my future family. Despite this amazing feat of spectacular daring, I eventually went on to have two children. Small miracles.

Of course, I realized high school was different. This was the real deal and would require the real equipment. So when the time came to take that step, I approached the horse-doored counter manned by a couple of senior students. Being freshmen, we were treated as second class citizens, so I was prepared for the requisite demeaning ridicule.

"I need a mouth guard, a small jockstrap and a cup," I said trying to look like I knew what I was doing. The student at the window turned to his assistant and said, "Hey, get this guy a mouth guard, a small jock and a peanut shell." His lackey buddy snickered at the personal slam and went looking for the goods. I cringed at his joke. I realize it was just a wise guy senior putting a lowly freshman in his proper place but, frankly, it stung a little. I'm guessing it's the equivalent of a girl being told she's flat chested, a real poke in the ego. The fact that I remember it from over forty years ago is testament to the power of words. Looking back, I recognize it was the beginning of a new chapter in my life, one that would be shaped by being in the company of largely boys and men for the next four years. The path was being lain for steeling myself against these kinds of masculinity attacks. It reeked of toxic masculinity before it was even a phrase.

I suddenly knew if I were going to succeed as a student, an athlete and eventually as a man, I would have to get used to both these gentle teases and in some cases, more pointed, critical assaults on my character. I'd have to suck it up and deal with them, case by case, situation by situation. Most every weakness you can think of was exposed under the microscope of an all-male school, perhaps foremost, whether you were a man or a wimp. I realize that, even today I struggle with releasing some of these conditioned notions of "real masculinity" where being sensitive, empathetic and compassionate are all viewed as weaknesses. Gifts from God that should be stifled in the name of acting like a man.

There wasn't much escaping it, either. High school boys can be pretty ruthless sometimes, and not having girls to keep them in check only made stereotypes and masculine expectations more pronounced. While we all came away from our high school experience with different perceptions of what it means to be a man, I sometimes wonder how my character would be different had there been a more pronounced female presence throughout those pivotal years. I think it helps having a balanced perspective, especially during those formative years, and that includes the feminine element. It softens everything.

***

In some respects, football practices meant more to me than the actual games. By week two of the season, I was already relegated to second, or sometimes third string receiver. This meant the probability of getting into a game was slim, so practices were my chance to actually see some action on the field. It meant nothing to anyone but me, but it was action nonetheless. It beat standing on the sidelines of every game waiting to get put in, knowing that, barring a locker room outbreak of E-coli, or a score of 63-0, there was not much chance of me playing.

For all the blood, sweat and tears of that year of freshman football, I can boil down the significant personal events of the season to exactly two. Neither of these moments fall within the 'catch the ball-score a touchdown-be a hero' expectations of that first day of equipment fitting either.

The first took place during a routine practice. I was in the huddle with the second team fronted by our second string quarterback, Dennis Kieger. He called a pass play that was to go to my side. Our offense was run-focused, so passes were a rare thing. Accordingly, this was the first and, as I recall, the only time I'd been called on to get the ball all year. I lined up and tried to look as nonchalant as possible so as to not tip my hand. The ball was snapped and I took off running my route, a quick down and out. Dennis winged the ball my way. I caught it and scampered my way for a couple of yards before being pulled down.

I hustled back to the huddle and Dennis said, "Nice catch, Landwehr. Way to go, baby." I wasn't sure who was more excited about the exchange, me or him. It was a benign play for all intents and purposes. But it was also one Dennis continued to bring up to me throughout the rest of the season. I'd helped make him look good and he was grateful for it. He was a nice guy and I was just happy to be in his good graces. Sad as it is to say, it was my finest hour. Or, maybe, thirty seconds.

The second incident was much more indicative of my entire freshman football experience, and it took place a few weeks later during practice on a scorching hot day in August. One of our drills had some of the second stringers stationed on the defensive side of the ball while the offense ran some plays at half speed. I was given a blocking pad and stood in as a linebacker. These pads are held in one arm and intended to give an offensive blocker a target to hit without the holder taking the entire hit.

I squared my stance and waited as each play developed. A couple of runs went to the opposite side from where I stood. Then, they ran one to my side. The quarterback handed the ball to the second back through. The blocking back, a mean, tough kid named Mark Jansen, came at me, blowing through the line at full speed, and hit me so hard my grandparents felt it. I sailed through the air, de-cleated and aloft, questioning my dedication to this godforsaken sport, before landing on my back on the grass. My helmet snapped backward and hit the ground like a tetherball on a string.

Jansen stood over me for a second and laughed a sinister laugh, "Heh, heh." This kid was known for being a hothead and looking for a fight. He had a rage and ruthlessness about him. I guess that's what made him such a good fit for a sport as violent as football. At the same time, the hit was overdone and out of place. Half-speed did not necessitate knocking the small kid on his butt. It was an intentional act of humiliation. Part of the game? Perhaps. Out of line? Probably.

I got up as quickly as I could to try to not appear rattled. I couldn't but help see some of the guys smirking and whispering about my abbreviated liftoff and crash landing. I probably would have done the same if it were someone else. But there is no doubt the hit was a turning point for me. I filed it away and later, among other things, it became the impetus for me to look toward other sports. A guy my size could get hurt. Add to that the fact I was pretty tired of sitting on the bench all year and it just seemed like time to pursue other sports. A single play had beaten the love of the game out of me, and I guess I have Jansen to thank for that come-to-Jesus moment.

The rest of the season went on about as I expected. We won some games, and lost a few. Through it all I learned there was simply no place for a 5'2" 110 pound kid on either side of the ball. I finished the year out anyway. I wasn't big, but I was no quitter. The following year, as I was hitchhiking home from school, my freshman coach, Mr. Kleinman picked me up. When I played under him, he was a fiery coach using such phrases as, "Remember boys, my favorite color is red," or, "I want you to be three things on this team. I want you to be agile, mobile, and Dadgom hostile!" We talked about normal life things during our short drive. It was a little weird to see a softer side of him as he drove me to my drop-off point. It was clear he didn't recognize me from the year before, so I brought up our joint history together.

"I actually played on your team last year," I said.

"You did? Well, there's a lot of guys I coach and teach, it's impossible to know them all," he said. I was a little surprised he didn't remember me, but he had a point, I guess.

"Are you playing JV this year?" he asked.

"No, I'm actually playing soccer, instead. I miss football, but am enjoying soccer too," I lied. Soccer was, and always will be, second fiddle to football for me.

"Well, that might be a better fit. Sometimes you gotta go with your heart."

"Yeah, I guess so,"

His few words that day were better than anything he'd ever taught me as a coach. They were words of advice with which I couldn't help but agree. As a coach, I don't believe he ever intentionally slighted us smaller kids. He was just doing what any coach would do, putting the best team on the field at any given time. In some sense my role among the benchwarmers and tackling dummies, set the stage for my experience playing soccer, a much better experience for me overall. And, for that, I owe him and the team a debt of thanks.

***

The other freshman sport I participated in was Track and Field. My interest began in middle school when we had a city-wide event. I took part in it for the St. Luke's team as a high jumper. Watching the Olympic athletes do the Fosbury Flop was fascinating to me. It was such an interesting, elegant technique executed by running in an arc toward the bar and then launching yourself off one foot, backward over a bar. After some initial success in the grade school practices and the track meet event, I committed to trying to master some version of it.

When track season rolled around, I tried out and made the team. Being I'd never really participated in an individual/team sport, I was introduced the idea of a personal best. As part of a team, you did your best to help the team to score points. The goal was always to come away with a team win. But, as Coach Bill Miles explained to me the idea of a personal best, track was a sport where, at the end of the day it came down to how you did personally. If you'd done a little better than your previous best, well, that was all you needed to worry about. In essence it was a bit of a life lesson. Try to do better every day.

As the weeks of practice wore on, I added the long jump to my repertoire. I still considered the high jump as my primary strength, but despite training diligently every practice, I struggled all year to make the starting height at meets. To qualify for moving on, athletes were required to clear a starting height of five feet, six inches.

While I struggled at hitting it, my freshman teammate Dan Fanth hit and exceed it every time. He had a natural ability and always seemed to float over the bar with ease. For him, five-six was just a warm up. I regularly cleared five feet, four inches, but that extra two inches seemed like a foot. It was a bit humiliating to have to sit out the rest of the event time and time again as I struggled to meet minimum height.

The season was long and personally sort of frustrating for me. The best I'd done was a third place finish in the long jump and fourth in the high. Naturally, I approached the last meet of the year with determination to make the starting height and see where I could go from there. My first two jumps were a continuation of the frustration I'd seen all year. On both, my trailing foot hit the bar and brought it down as I flopped onto the landing mats. After my second miss, I waited as the rest of the non-qualifying jumpers took their final turn. Like many individual sports much of the preparation is mental. I am my own worst critic and I knew it, so I tried to focus on just doing my best and not on my previous two failures. It seemed I was jumping with a monkey on my back, and I wanted it off.

Dan Fanth strolled over after my second miss. "Hey Jim, I watched your last couple of jumps and your right leg isn't getting high enough on your launch. Give it a good kick when you go off your left."

"Huh. That makes sense. I'll give it a shot. Thanks, man."

While I'd trained all season with Dan, our jumping techniques were personal affairs. He seemed to have natural lift and grace. My own were more ungainly attempts. I was a high jump try-hard inflicted with slightly bad form and cheap shoes. I loved the sport though and was determined to give it one hundred percent all season.

The judge called my name and I stepped up to my starting point. With Dan's advice fresh in my mind, I looked toward the bar, a short, arc-shaped run from where I stood. After a final cleansing breath I loped toward the bar. When I reached the launch point, I kicked my right leg up toward my chest. I kicked my right leg up with force, then arched my back and finished with kicking my legs as I floated over the bar.

I looked up expecting to see the bar laying on the ground as I'd seen all season. Instead, it sat perched between the two standards, unaffected by my jump. I'd done it! I cleared starting height! Trying to contain my excitement at such a benign achievement, I walked over to my teammates. Dan congratulated me and said, "Nice jump, Jim. Hey, your nose is bleeding."

"Oh, thanks. Yeah, I think I hit it with my knee as I launched."

I shrunk away and tilted my head back, trying to stave off the bleeding. I went over to a grassy area and lay down. After a couple of minutes the bleeding stopped and I started thinking about my next jump. The bar was moved up to five feet eight. What were the chances I could best a personal best? In typical fashion, I laughed off the thought. Self-confidence was something that would need to be earned one meet, one jump at a time. Such is the struggle of an individual sport athlete where most of the pressure to perform comes from within. It's you against you.

I gave it my best but managed to miss all three of my next attempts. It didn't matter to me at this point. I'd beaten back the demons of self-doubt and set a new personal best that day. And while it was nothing to write home about, it was good enough for me. Sometimes in life these small achievements are all we need to push us further around the track.

Outside of this personal best, the sum total of my track season accomplishments that year was those third and fourth place ribbons earned in a meet earlier that year. As a young man who was all about the trophy and the tangible recognition of achievement, these stupid little ribbons meant a lot. I hung them on my bulletin board in my bedroom as proof I was kind of halfway good at a couple of track events on one specific day in my life. They were menial awards that came with qualifiers and disclaimers, but they were MY awards. They represented the entire breadth of my hours of practice and training. While most people would likely shove them in a drawer somewhere, I needed to see them to remind me what I was capable of, or maybe more importantly, how far I needed yet to go. Reminders of how life is not always made up of blue ribbons and the top of the podium. Sometimes it's comprised of fourth place ribbons and bloody noses.

***

After my physically punishing year in football as a freshman, I opted to change gears sophomore year and try my hand at soccer. I'd never played it before and it seemed like a better fit given my height and weight. Plus, Brother Walter was coach and he was a likeable guy. My friend Michael Baker, a neighbor from across the street, was the one who ultimately convinced me to play. He was a gifted athlete and an all-round soccer nut. On any given day of the summer you could find him out in the street juggling a ball with his feet, sometimes for minutes on end.

In addition to being a nice guy, Brother Walter was a pretty good coach. He was fair, fun and he tried to play everyone at some point in most every game. He had a good understanding of strategy and, as a result, we won more than we lost. One thing that drove him absolutely crazy however was what he called "bunching." It is a natural phenomenon in soccer where the ball serves as a magnet for position players looking to get a little action. It was an attractant and led to swarms of guys all looking to get their kicks in. Hence, bunching.

So when this happened, and it happened every game and every practice, Brother would scream from the sidelines, "Open space, open space! You're bunching!" It was his attempt to get the three guys hanging around the ball to spread out so the guy dribbling had options on who he could pass it to. As a player though, there was little fun in playing away from the ball in hopes someone might pass it to you. So we swarmed the ball like bees, and Brother Walter shouted in vain.

About a third of the way through the season, Brother wanted to address an issue he'd seen with many of us on the team. It seems we had a habit of flinching and turning away from the attacker at critical moments of defense. This is not only bad defense, it looks bad from the sidelines. One should square up and attack the attacker, not wince and turn sideways.

After Brother had seen enough of this, he told us all to bring a bandana to the next practice. At the end of practice he instructed us to grab our bandanas, cover our eyes with them and get in a line. He went up to the first guy in the line, Kerry Casey, and gently threw the ball at his chest.

"Did that hurt, Mr. Casey?"

"No."

Brother threw the ball at his thigh and asked, "How about that? Did that hurt?"

"Nope."

Then on to the next guy. Another chest shot. "Did that hurt Mr. Krogh?"

"Not really."

Brother then went down the line and did similar sequences to the rest of us. His point was coming across loud and clear. It was a sadistic sort of teachable moment. The point he was driving home was that to play good defense we needed to conquer our fear of the very thing we were trying to acquire, namely, the ball. It was a decent technique, albeit unnerving not knowing when or where the ball was going to hit me when my turn came around. When he reached the end of the line, Brother said, "I think we're seeing a pattern here, don't you agree gentlemen?"

"Yes, coach!" the team responded. In my opinion, we all played a little more aggressively after that practice.

***

Being new to soccer, I was not good enough to be a starter on the sophomore team. I was a solid second stringer though, and got a decent amount of playing time over the course of the season. Most of it just consisted of a whole lot of running, but there were a couple of high points.

One was during a game against Saint Paul Academy, a rival high school from down the street. I was playing as a midfielder, attacking when I could and defending when necessary. At one point in the game one of their players hit the ball with their arm inside the goal area causing a penalty and a stoppage of play. Our team was granted a penalty kick. Brother Walter shouted, "Hey, Landwehr, take the penalty kick!"

I was a bit shocked at the declaration, in part because I'd never been asked to do something significant in all my days in any sport uniform. A penalty kick was huge, because it was a one-on-one shootout with the goaltender, while the rest of both teams stood and watched. The goalie was not allowed to move until contact was made with the ball, so the kicker had a decent advantage. It was not quite a sure thing, but close.

The referee set the ball at the penalty kick spot and backed away. The goaltender took his position and waited for the whistle. When it was blown, I took my three step approach and blasted a shot toward the goal. The goaltender dove in front of the ball and made a save. I was as surprised as he was. My ego was immediately deflated, as pretty much anyone should be able to make a penalty kick. I turned and started jogging back toward the middle of the field.

Before long, I heard people shouting, "Landwehr! Hey, Landwehr, you get another try!" I turned around and saw the referee waving in my direction. When I got back to him, he said the goalie had moved prior to the kick, a violation resulting in another opportunity for me. I was shocked, but welcomed the chance at redemption.

I realigned myself at the penalty kick line as the goaltender got set. I was determined to score this time. The whistle blew, I took a breath, started my approach, and burned another shot toward the goal. It was a frozen rope that hit midway up the back of the net to the right of the goalie.

Gggggooooooaaaaalllll! I scored a flippin' goal! I scored, everyone!

My teammates erupted and a few even came up and congratulated me. I tried to play it cool, like I'd done this before, but on the inside, I was all aflutter. There's nothing much cooler than actually scoring points for your team. Oh sure, there's ten other guys all helping in other ways, but at the end of the day it is the guys who get the ball in the goal that ensure the team's success. We went on to win that game. And while I didn't score the rest of the season, I'd had my little moment on the podium, and it made up for all the long practices and any doubts about whether soccer was a better choice than football as a sophomore.

CHAPTER 14: DRIVING

I never knew I was a bad driver until I got married. Now I am reminded of it daily by not only my wife, but my grown children. My wife is one who is quick to reach for the door handle when she feels her safety is threatened, which apparently happens every ten minutes when I am behind the wheel. My kids point out my rolling stops at stop-signs and my yellow light, speed-up-and-run-throughs with a sarcastic, "Really, dad?" It's weird because I never feel unsafe at any time when I'm driving, except maybe because of the rest of the maniacs on the road out there. Whatever the case, I owe all of my skills, or lack thereof, to a guy known as, Driver Ed.

Yes, it's true, our driver's education instructor's name, ironically enough, was Ed. This created the running joke for years at Cretin that you took Driver's Ed from Driver Ed. His normal post was head librarian, but in the fall and spring he taught driver's training and behind-the-wheel for a couple of hours after school or on weekends. It was there we were taught the basics of traffic laws using written materials and bad training videos from the 60's. This included the mandatory bloody highway movie that was shown to evoke fear into our reckless driving heads. When the required number of class time hours had been met, we were allowed to take our learner's permit test. If we passed, we could start our behind the wheel training.

Ed had another unfortunate nickname. We called him Sweaty Eddie. He was a nervous, twitchy guy with a propensity for sweating. This was likely one of the job hazards of training pubescent maniacs to drive a two-ton killing machine. Ed's short sleeve print shirts were often times pitted-out, while his brow glistened with beads of perspiration. I cannot say I blame him one iota for his affliction. I am certain my hours spent driving him around the city were the source of a stomach ulcer or two for Mr. Ed.

One of the perks of being a driver's education instructor was being given the use of a new car to train students in. It was certainly counterintuitive but it was the least they could do for the poor teachers relegated to the jump seat. Driver Ed used a brand new, burgundy Ford Granada for his behind the wheel training. When they were first produced, these cars were touted on TV commercials as having a ride as comfortable as a Mercedes Benz. This was Ford Motor Company's laughable claim intended to woo the middle class. It's hard to think of a car further away from a Mercedes at the time.

My friend Pat took his training with Ed a few months before me. During an attempt at parallel parking, he got a little too close to the curb and mutilated a hubcap, thereby validating my questioning the use of new vehicles. In my opinion students should be trained in something closer to the type of auto that would be their first car. I'm thinking one with no hubcaps, a bad muffler and a glove box that won't stay closed. Besides, there's a certain healthy level of comfort that comes with driving more of a beater.

We were required to complete twelve hours of training with half of those being a back seat observer while the poor schlep in the driver's seat took instructions and berating at the hands of Ed. My stints behind the wheel with Sweaty Eddie were angst-ridden affairs for both of us. As a safety measure, the training cars were equipped with a passenger side brake pedal that students called the "chicken brake." This pedal was seen as a last resort for the instructor to avoid getting in an accident. It was a goal of all students to get through their training without having Ed hit the chicken brake on them.

I wish I could say I was one of those students.

On my first outing one Saturday morning we were driving around the city of Saint Paul and things were going well. Driver Ed gave frequent updates and instructions as we picked our way through both busy and residential streets.

"Watch your speed here. Take a left up here at the light. Check your mirrors," he said as we travelled around willy-nilly. As I approached a light somewhere in Falcon Heights he said, "Turn right at the next light."

I signaled and slowed. I began my turn when suddenly Ed shouted, "Hey, hey, hey!" and the car skidded to a stop. Our heads bobbed forward as we reacted to the quick stop. Ed chicken braked me!

"What did I do?"

"You see that guy in the crosswalk? He has the right of way! You almost hit him."

Sure enough, there was a gentleman standing in the crosswalk looking at me in disbelief. He'd come from across the street where I'd neglected to look.

"Oops, sorry about that," I said as Ed politely waved the guy across.

"You need to approach these crosswalks with caution, Jim."

I nodded, apologized again and let the guy cross before I continued on down the road. And so it had begun. I was barely forty five minutes into my behind the wheel time and I'd already been chicken braked. I was out of Driver Ed's good graces right out of the gate. The worst part was I'd lost his confidence. If the instructor has to essentially pull the ripcord for your first jump out of the plane, well, you would be well served to prepare to feel that pull again.

And feel it I did.

Ed hit the chicken brake twice more in the remaining five lessons I had. For those keeping score at home, that is three out of six. Fifty percent! Basically, every other time I got in the car with him he "chickened out." Were both of those other two justified? Probably, although one was contestable, as it was a confusing approach off of Shepard Road. Or, at least confusing to me.

When we came to a stop after my final lesson, he took a moment in the car to offer his assessment.

"Well, Jim, you still need *a lot* of practice before you test for your license. You have some tendencies that aren't real good and don't have a good feel for the vehicle. You tend to drift lanes and you need a lot more work on your turns. This is all stuff that will get better with more practice, but I don't want to give you false confidence you're ready for your exam yet, because you need a lot more practice."

Well, it was apparent there wasn't much good to build on, from what he'd said. It was a sobering talk, but one I needed to hear. I was determined to prove him wrong, get my practice driving in and pass the exam.

***

I sat nervously in the driver's seat in line at the start of the driver's license test course while my sister Jane waited inside the Department of Motor Vehicles building, a short walk away. My shoulder muscles were tight and the pit of my stomach filled with dread as I awaited the next available exam official. The test staff were dressed in khaki dress pants and light blue shirts and ties, giving them a daunting militaristic or police-like appearance. My days at Cretin had given me an understanding of the respect a uniform garnered, but didn't alleviate the uneasiness of seeing these men and women. They represented judge and jury at this, the trial of my driving skills. And judging from my behind the wheel experience, I was a student without a public defender.

The test courses in Minnesota were closed courses constructed with the intention of throwing as many situations at the new driver as possible within the confines of a compact series of streets. The course had one-ways, yields, stop signs and stoplights, speed limit changes and the much-dreaded parallel parking section. There were signs everywhere you looked. In fact, Driver Ed even warned me the test was almost over-signed, to the point of causing confusion. The course was a mini-city riddled with laws and ride-along cops to see you obeyed every one of them.

After an unnerving ten minute wait, a test official came up to my window and asked my name. After confirming it, he got in the passenger seat. "Okay, James, today we are going to take a run through the entire course. Before each maneuver, I will be instructing you as to what I want you to do. Depending on how well you carry out those maneuvers, I will be detracting points from your total score. You must score at least a seventy to pass. If you break any traffic laws, it will result in an automatic failure, of course."

Of course.

He asked if I had any questions and, after I replied no, he told me to pull out and take an immediate right turn. I shifted the Plymouth into drive, signaled a right turn and inched my way into the two lane road. It was clear I'd nailed my first maneuver. I accelerated slowly up the road. Halfway down the block the tester told me to take a left at the next intersection. Sensing he was trying to test my savvy with the old one way street trick right out of the gate, I anticipated his deceit by turning the car into the nearest lane, with the curb just outside my driver's side tire.

Nailed that one too.

The instructor started writing and then spoke up, "Okay, please pull over to the right. You've just failed the exam."

"What? What did I do?" I asked in disbelief.

"See that car up ahead?" he asked pointing down the road.

"Yes, sir?"

"Well, that is another student testing and you happen to be in his lane. Please pull over to the right and park, James."

Oh, my God this can't be happening. I just started!

I signaled and pulled over to allow him to document the details of what might qualify as the quickest exam failure in his career. I doubt the vehicle ever hit more than fifteen miles per hour before it was condemned to stop. He scribbled and scrawled for a minute or so, and then started his lecture.

"James, I'm failing you today for breaking a traffic law. Driving in the wrong lane is a serious violation and is an automatic failure. I will allow you to continue the rest of the exam in order to give you some practice, but just know you did fail today."

Yeah, I think you said that. A couple times now, in fact.

I felt deflated. At sixteen years old, all any kid wants is to pass his driver's test and be granted the freedom of the road. Now it would have to wait. Furthermore, there was the embarrassment of having to tell my family and friends I'd failed a test most of them passed in their first attempt. I was never a kid beaming with confidence, and things like this only served to tear me down a bit further. I reasoned I would just have to buck up and deal with it. I swore I would do better next time, though it wouldn't take much to get further along in the test than I did today.

***

My other sister, Pat, accompanied me on my second attempt at the driver's exam. On our way to the testing center, she coached me all the way about checking mirrors, keeping my hands at the ten and two position, complete stops, etc. The pressure was on and I was a nervous wreck and despite her good intentions, the coaching wasn't reducing the anxiety level at all. I'd heard of people failing the exam three and four times, but I was determined to keep it to one.

I pulled up to the starting point and Pat wished me luck as she exited and went into the examination building. I sat their waiting alone, left to sweat it out behind the wheel. The examination official, a different gentleman from the first test, buckled himself in, went over the guidelines and gave me the go ahead to start. I took an immediate right and when we approached the fateful intersection, he said, "Okay,

James, take a left at the next intersection." This time I held my lane and executed the turn perfectly.

Aha! Take that sucker! Fool me once…

The official seemed unfazed by the sense of confidence I felt having exorcised this demon from my past. I drove on.

The two of us travelled the turns of the closed course over the next ten minutes, left, right, left. When we got to the dreaded parallel parking maneuver, I signaled and swung the Plymouth into the spot without touching the guideposts. It was another confidence-builder as it was well-known that if you hit one of the posts, it was an automatic failure. The official scratched some numbers onto the test form and told me to pull out and resume the test.

I signaled, checked my mirrors, eased the car back onto the course and continued driving. We took a couple of simple turns and ended up on a three lane, one way street – something I've rarely ever encountered in my forty years of driving – but here it was. He instructed me to move over to the far left lane, so I signaled, checked my mirror and over my shoulder and eased the car over.

"Okay, take a left up at the next intersection, James."

As I approached the turn, my mind was in one-way-land. I was obsessed with these traffic aberrations and their dream-killing potential. Assuming this was another one way, I turned into the near lane and proceeded. When I saw the centerline was yellow, not white, I panicked. "Is this a one-way street?" I asked.

"Please pull over to the right, James. You've just failed the exam."

Oh my God, are you kidding me? Again?

It was clear he wasn't giving any mulligans or do-overs on this day. Once again, I pulled the car over feeling defeated, like a complete and total idiot. How could I possibly fail an exam twice by turning into the wrong lane? What sort of oncoming traffic disability was I afflicted with that would subject me to embarrassing humiliation twice within a two-week period? In the Knucklehead School of Driving, I was top of the class.

He proceeded to explain to me what I already knew, about how driving the wrong way down a street is dangerous and grounds for an automatic failure.

Yep. I got it, dude. Done it. Twice now as a matter of fact. But, thanks.

When I returned to the examination building, my sister got in the car and said, "So, how did you do, Jimbo?"

"Not so good. Failed again."

"Again, really? Why this time?"

"Same thing. Turning left into the oncoming traffic lane."

Pat covered her mouth and stifled a little giggle. Only a sibling can find a sliver of humor in the depths of another sibling's failure. At the same time, her attitude took the edge off the seriousness of the situation. It helped me realize while this was a disappointment, it also wasn't the end of the world. In fact it was the reason people are tested in the first place, to work these kinds of "snafus" out. We both knew I would pass eventually, but until I did, we had a good laugh at me and my multiple-offender status.

When Mom found out I had failed again, she ratcheted up my behind-the-wheel training by invoking the help of my brother Tom. For all intents and purposes, he was the father-figure around the house and, by now, she was out of ideas. Tom took me out a few times around the city and drilled me on the basics again and again, building my confidence one turn at a time.

He accompanied me to the test for my third attempt. On our way there he kept telling me to relax. Recognizing I had nothing to lose at this point, I did relax and it seemed to make the test simpler, more intuitive. It might also have had to do with the fact I was significantly more familiar with the course at this point. When I got to the end, the official informed me I'd passed with a score of eighty-something. I was both ecstatic and relieved.

I still feel Tom's advice on relaxing made all the difference between passing and failing. It was a lesson that, sometimes life is easier when we stop stressing about the rules and laws, and just relax. At the same time, despite having my license now for forty years without a major event, I am still frequently reminded by my wife and kids that I could still use a lot more practice.

CHAPTER 15: VICES

It was New Year's Eve, 1976. As a sophomore, I had no plans, intent on spending the night at home. My mom and her boyfriend, Jack, typically rented a hotel room in Hudson, Wisconsin for their New Year's Eve celebration. This left the house open as a hosting place for sibling parties, disorderly conduct and chaos. Some might call this negligence on the part of my mom, but I beg to differ. She worked hard all year, and earned that night out to celebrate the passing of another year without a nervous breakdown. Besides, most of us were old enough to care for ourselves, giving her a much needed break from the rigors of single parenthood.

Unlike me, my siblings were off at various events. Pat had moved out of the house by then, Jane was out with friends, and Rob and Paul were both at friends' for overnights, leaving just Tom and me at home in the early evening. I was a homebody prepared to spend the night alone watching Laurel and Hardy's, *The Music Box*, an annual tradition on New Year's Eve television. That would be followed by Johnny Carson until midnight, then bed. Yes, I really knew how to have a good time. It's true.

Like the rest of the family, Tom had plans to go out with friends as well. He regularly haunted Paul's Bar, where he played pool and talked smart with a couple of his buddies. This New Year's was no different.

As an evening pre-game warm up, Tom cracked a beer and put his new Doc Watson album, *Memories* on the stereo. Watson was a blind musician who played a mixture of folk, Americana and blues. He was an ultra-talented guitar and banjo player and always had a capable backing band. As a teen, I was a rock and roller, so this music was foreign to me, but I quickly developed an ear for it. There was something refreshingly simplistic about it. The rhythm and strumming of his guitar, accompanied by the happy little lyrics of "Shady Grove" sort of carried me away. In my youth I was exposed to Johnny Cash's music in the likes of, "A Boy Named Sue," which was the closest thing

I could equate to this wonderful music. It made me think of someone sitting on a porch in Carolina pluckin' and singin'.

"Hey, Jimbo, you want a beer?" Tom asked.

The question caught me off guard. I was only fifteen at the time and the legal drinking age was nineteen. It seemed so shamefully wrong, yet so enticingly risky, I had to double check.

"Uh, are you sure?"

"Sure! Heck, it's what all the other sophomore boys are out doing tonight." His logic seemed like a bit of a stretch, but if he was buying, I guess I was drinking.

"Uh, okay."

"It's in the fridge, help yourself."

I wandered into the kitchen, opened up the refrigerator and grabbed a Pabst Blue Ribbon. I popped it open and took a swig of the carbonated swill. Its bitterness washed down my throat causing me to finish with a wince. I still wasn't sure what the appeal of beer was. I'd had tastes of my stepfather's beer in the past and thought it was disgusting. Pop at least had a fruitiness and sweetness to it, whereas beer just didn't seem to have much going for it in the flavor department. Based on everything I'd seen and heard though, it was the pathway to unbridled fun, social popularity and success, so I figured it was worth a good old high school try.

Deep down, I also knew it led to tragedies like the undoing of Kerouac and Hemingway, along with countless broken homes and broken lives. But I drank my first real PBR nonetheless. The only way to figure out what the great allure was, was to try it, right?

In order to impress my big brother, I slammed the beer in ten minutes, lest I be perceived as a wimp. When I went to throw away the can, Tom said, "Have another one, Jimbo. Or two or three. It's New Year's, after all!

Having choked down the first one, I grabbed another and strolled back out to the living room. Doc Watson's wailing voice on the song, "Walkin' Boss" echoed around the living room as I plunked myself on the couch.

"Walkin' Boss, Walkin' Boss. Yes, you're the boss. But I don't belong to you."

As I worked my way through the second beer, I was beginning to feel Doc's angst about working for the man. The crisp notes and his soulful vocals with a little help from the suds made me reflective and appreciative of the songwriting talents of Doc. He was singing about a railroad worker standing up to his boss, but the lyrics seemed to take on more significance after a PBR shot to the head. My brain was beginning to feel the effects of the brew in a way I had not expected. I was more relaxed and my initial worry about underage drinking kind of vanished.

For amusement, I banged away on a tabletop pinball game one of us kids had received as a Christmas gift. It was one of those cheap units that ran on batteries and took away precious hours of your life in the name of dinging, buzzing and personal high scores. I chugged through my second beer, impressed with my building pinball savvy.

I finished my beer and went for another. It was approaching nine o'clock and Tom was getting ready to head out with his friends. "Jimbo, I'm taking off. I'll leave you a couple more beers if you want them."

"Yeah! Sounds good, thanks," I said. I had nothing but time to finish out the year, and more beer seemed like it would help ring in the new. It seemed one beer greased the skids for an invitation to another, much like it probably had for Hemingway and Kerouac. I was on my first drinking binge and I didn't even know it. I did know I was feeling good and any nagging worries and anxieties from sophomore year were melting away with every ounce.

Tom left, the door slammed and I was alone. It was kind of pathetic really, drinking alone on New Year's Eve with little to look forward to but a black and white Laurel and Hardy movie. Here was another fine mess I'd gotten myself into. At the same time, I was always happiest alone, so this made perfect sense. I was harming no one but myself and as long as I didn't make a habit of drinking alone I'd be okay.

I finished my third and fourth beers and hammered away at the flippers as Doc Watson sang songs about trains and jail. I was really digging this guy and was on the second play of his entire double album. By the time I cracked the fifth beer, I was pleasantly buzzed and a little bored. I flipped on the television and tuned into the middle of the Music Box. I grinned and occasionally laughed out loud as Laurel and Hardy struggled with the piano. Even movies took on a different feel after a few beers. Ordinary stuff seemed funnier and more absurd than when I was sober.

At 10:30 Johnny Carson came on and I switched channels to watch. I always liked his show, but it was on too late so I typically only watched it on Friday nights. There is nothing better at killing a good buzz than a talk show, so within twenty minutes I fell asleep. Passed out.

The next thing I remember was my sister Jane shaking me awake at 1:00 am.

"Jimmy, Jimmy wake up."

I opened my eyes and wondered what day it was and how I'd ended up asleep on the couch. *I never sleep on the couch. What the heck?* I sat up, then slowly stood up and rocked back and forth heel to toe once. I stared quizzically at Jane through my PBR beer goggles.

"What were you doing?" she asked.

"I um. Heh, heh. I was, um, just watching Johnny Carson and I must have fallen asleep," I said, swaying and sloshing like a teenage Foster Brooks.

Sensing something was not normal, Jane asked, "Jimmy, are you drunk?"

"Um, no, no, no. I'm fine. I'm fine. Well, maybe a little," I said. My head spun. I'd been found out, but I didn't much care at the moment. I only knew I wanted to go back to sleep, whatever year it was.

Jane laughed. "I can't believe my little brother Jimmy is drunk."

"It's true, I think. I'm fine. I'm gonna go to bed now."

Jane switched off the television and asked, "Where did you get the beer?"

"Tom gave me a few," I said.

"Well, I hope mom doesn't find out," she said with a conniving grin. Leave it to your sister to plant that seed of fear in you before your head hits the pillow for the night. Jane was good at messing with your mind, but rarely followed through on threats of exposure or tattling. She was cool that way.

I stumbled my way up to bed and began 1977 drunk as a skunk.

***

The next morning I was awoken by Jane. She opened my bedroom door and said, "Jimmy, get up! It's time to take down the tree and the Christmas stuff."

Jane shut the door and went back downstairs.

I opened my eyes and my brain sloshed in my skull and throbbed like there was a tiny bass drummer inside pounding out notes, thump, thump! My stomach didn't feel quite a hundred percent either as it worked itself into a low roil. I was in the throes of my first real hangover and it was hitting me like the Wabash Cannonball train Doc Watson sang about last night. I thought to myself, *if this is what a hangover is like, I'll never drink again!*

My mouth started to water the way it only does when you know you're about to experience a sudden unexpected weight loss. *Uh oh, here it comes! Fire in the hole!*

I turned and rushed upstairs to the bathroom. I knelt by the toilet bowl and retched, paying homage to King Kohler the porcelain god of gastronomic expulsion and unscheduled purges. I retched a second and third time as I surrendered to my body's self-cleanse. As I knelt there wondering if there was to be another round, I heard Jane shout from downstairs, "Jimmy, hurry up or I'll have to tell mom our little secret!"

I'll never drink again. I promise, God. Just get me through this day.

It was then the Doc Watson ear worm started. "Walkin' boss. Walkin' boss."

Oh, dear God, not that song again. I suddenly hated beer, pinball, Laurel and Hardy, Johnny Carson and most of all, Doc Watson. The song made me think of Pabst Blue Ribbon, which in turn made me remember how many I'd had. That reminder made me retch again, this time mostly a dry heave.

Oh, dear Lord, help me. I think I'm dying.

After a few more moments of spitting and existential soul-searching, I managed to rise to my feet and head downstairs to face the wrath of my older sister. One of mom's directives before leaving for her New Year's celebration was that we were to take down the tree and all the Christmas decorations before she got home. Jane was in charge of the oversight and took her job seriously. And when she was in a mood, her words were like God's own thunder to us younger boys. On this first day of 1977, she wore that mood like a coat of arms.

When she saw me, she grinned at me and said, "How are you feeling this morning?"

"Not too good."

"Well, too bad, we've got a lot to do, so start taking those decorations off the tree and putting them in their boxes."

I moved with tentativeness and sloth, as everything seemed to be a struggle. When you drop a cluster bomb like five PBR's on your brain at the age of fifteen, evidently it affects your entire central nervous system. I picked ornament after ornament off, trying to get the job done so I could go back to bed. This chore was my penance, the price I needed to pay for my iniquities, and it was killing me. At the moment, Jane was my Walkin' Boss, and I *did* belong to her. Ten minutes into my work, I felt feverish and my mouth began to water again, a telltale sign it was time to pay a repeat visit to worship King Kohler. I raced upstairs and hurled once more.

As I knelt next to the bowl with the smell of vomit fresh in my nasal cavities, an inner voice in my head shouted over the earworm din of Doc Watson's banjo playing, *I swear, I am never drinking again!*

After a couple more dry heaves, I gathered myself together, despite a throbbing head and intermittent sweats. Early indications were this drinking thing came at a great price. I wasn't sure I was up to the task. Right now though, I had to check in with my Walkin' Boss before she got angry enough to rat me out to our mother. I stood and made my way back downstairs.

Jane looked at me with a wide grin and said, "Drinking is fun, isn't it?"

"Ugh. Yeah, real fun."

It seemed she was enjoying her role as parent in Mom's stead. I resumed taking decorations off the tree. As I did, I began trying to count how many beers I'd had the night before. It was at least five, maybe six. I couldn't recall. This morning however, the mere thought of the word Pabst made my stomach flip-flop. I was conflicted because I recalled the elation and sense of high I felt nine hours prior, but was now at death's door brought on by the same thing that caused the elation. After I finished removing the decorations, I took the tree out of the stand and dragged it out to the alley for pickup. I then went back to bed to sleep off the rest of my first hangover.

While I was probably younger than most, my first drunk was probably similar to most peoples'. As first timers, we enter these situations feeling adult-sized invincibility but are ill-prepared for the consequences. Alcohol makes a teenager feel grown up and powerful. It temporarily heals the awkwardness of adolescence and each drink numbs a little of that. I know for at least an hour on that New Year's Eve, I was the table top Pin Ball Wizard. I also felt like I was expanding my world just a little using Pabst as my drug of choice while listening to the Folk-Americana music of Doc Watson. The realities of my life were softer. Life, as it seemed in those moments, was pretty good.

But on that New Year's Day, I'd also learned a valuable lesson about over-imbibing. The fun came at a price. And, needless to say, I did not stay true to my promise of never drinking again. No one ever does. Furthermore, I was a slow learner as the coming years would prove. This event was a stepping stone into a controlled wildness that was my teens and early twenties. I skated onto this thin ice of risk and recklessness more frequently than I should have, but I wouldn't change a thing. Sometimes teens thrash and flounder en route to adulthood, and looking back, I was no different. I'll confess, it was quite a while before I could listen to Doc Watson again without a nasty flashback. But I recognize that night drinking alone with help from the voice and guitar of a blind musician was all part of my journey to who I was to become.

***

Several of our Friday nights during senior year were spent looking to do something on the edge of legality. I cannot explain why, but I have a notion it has everything to do with the journey from being a kid who is told what to do for their whole life, to an autonomous, free-thinking young adult. There is also something incredibly alluring about reaching the ages of doing things considered adult. When we were sixteen, it was the right to drive. At seventeen, it was the ability to get into an R-rated movie. Eighteen, meant the right to vote. And the holy grail of adulthood, nineteen, which meant we could legally drink alcoholic beverages. As teens we spent a lot of time looking toward growing older and the alleged benefits and freedoms therein.

So, as I approached the tail end of my teen years, my divergence from the straight-and-narrow stemmed from a few factors. First, I was always considered the "good kid" in the family. Mom used to say I was the one that never gave her an ounce of trouble. While this statement was flattering, it was also a brand or a labeling I hated and spent most of my high school years trying to refute. The cool, popular kids like Kevin Galligan, Dino Joyce and Tom Orput didn't have much time for the goodie-goodies like me. So, I spent significant effort proving to myself and my friends that I was capable of coloring outside the lines on occasion. Furthermore, most of my older siblings had a wild edge to them, so I had a legacy to sustain as well.

Another factor in this shift in risk was simply the angst of growing up. On top of all the physiological and hormonal changes we grappled with, our frontal lobes were not yet developed enough to make rational, mature decisions. Attempting to distance ourselves from the dependency of our parents, we were driven forward by our young energy and unfounded illusions of invincibility.

Every Friday at school, word got around about where the party was, who was hosting and other important specifics like whether there would be girls and beer. There were at least three well-known party spots among the Cretin crowd. First, there was "The Monument." This was code for the bluffs of the Mississippi River at the end of Summit Avenue where a large concrete Civil War monument stood giving the party spot its name. And, though I never attended one, there were frequent keggers held in the brush of the river bluffs as well as down on the shore of the river.

A highly popular spot for a time was "The Caves," a series of large natural caverns cut into the limestone banks of the Mississippi. Their purpose at one time was for aging beer for the local Schmidt brewery. During my underclass years I was never brave enough to try to hang out at any of these places. But as I grew older I thought I should probably knock a couple off my list to at least know what the cool kids were talking about.

After hearing a lot of buzz around school about the Caves, Pete, Dan, Pat, Doug and I decided we would make a trip to check them out on a Friday night. I picked them up in Mom's Volare' about eight o'clock in the evening. We swung by the Super America gas station and sent Pete in to see if he could score some beer. At the time, the only beer sold at gas stations was "3.2." Short for 3.2% alcohol, it is the weak, watered down version of the regular "strong" beer. It was the product of Minnesota's conservative foundation. If you were crazy enough to drink it trying to get drunk, well, good luck to you. If you succeeded, you were setting yourself up for what was known as the 3-2 flu; a good old cheap beer hangover. Because it was also the only alcohol sold after liquor stores closed at 10:00 PM and on Sundays, when they were closed altogether, it was a product of desperation. But it always seemed to work in a pinch or in our case as a spelunking beverage of choice. Frankly, any beer we could get using deceit and persuasion was good enough.

Pete came walking back to the car with a twelve pack of Miller High life in his grasp. He got in and said, "Score, boys!"

"You the man, Pete!" I exclaimed.

"They card you or give you any grief?" Pat asked.

"Nope. Sometimes, you just have to look like you know what you're doing."

Pat went in next and purchased a pack of Swisher Sweet cigars, because nothing makes a cave experience more gratifying than cheap beer and cigars that taste like old socks. It was clear that even if there were girls in these caves, and there likely would not be, we would repulse them with our tobacco-tainted auras and ill-gotten suds. Nope, this was all boys right here. It was our subterranean adventure. I'm a coal miner, dude!

With the goods in our possession, we were ready to go. We made our way toward the caves. Pete knew the approximate entrance point on Shepard Road. When we got there, I parked the car and we started prepping for our descent into the unknown. Everyone packed a couple of beers into their coats for safekeeping. We each put a candle in our pocket while Pat secured the stogies and the lighter. As high school adventurists, we were good to go. All that was missing was a case of black lung, and the Swisher Sweets would take care of that nicely.

After checking traffic to ensure no one was watching, we crossed the road and hiked down the trail leading into the wooded bluffs. A few yards down the trail we came to what we determined to be the entrance. It was a ridiculously small hole cut into the limestone hillside, one that made all of us pause and wonder if we really wanted to pursue this little thrill.

"This is it?" Pat said with a hint of a laugh.

"I guess so, yeah. Must be," Pete answered.

"Wow. Well, who wants to go first?" Pat asked.

"I'm shortest, so I'll go," Pete offered.

He crouched down and crawled into the opening, careful not to bang his bottles of Miller on the limestone walls in the process. Pete wriggled and writhed his way until we couldn't see him anymore. Pat went next and Dan and I followed. It was a human chain of chance in a tunnel to the great unknown. We couldn't resist its allure.

Having no light source yet, we were enveloped in darkness. As I worked my way down the narrow tunnel, I became acutely aware of how confining the spaces were. The fact that we were one small rock fall or cave-in from being buried alive was not lost on me. None of our parents really knew where any of us were. Earlier, we all lied to them all about where we were going. Because, nothing would get you grounded for life faster than saying, "Yeah, Mom, I'm gonna go out with my buddies, pick up some beer and a few cigars and crawl into some perilous caves that were supposed to have been sealed up years ago. Is that alright with you?"

Instead, it was more like, "I'm going to go hang out with Pat, Pete, Dan and Doug tonight."

In a cave.

When I reached the main chamber, Pete and the others were waiting. They all had their candles lit and were marveling at the height of the ceiling. I grabbed mine and I lit it using Pat's flame. We held our candles high and craned our necks to see the limestone magnificence of our new confines. It was an enormous natural structure with ceilings twenty feet or higher. It was a perfect location for beer that demanded a constant temperature for lagering.

Down here, we were clearly in the belly of the beast. The air was stale and humid, acrid with a smoky tinge to it. The floor was sandy and littered with bottles, cardboard twelve-pack containers and other trash left behind from previous revelers. Pat joked about how ironic it was this cave once used to ferment and store beer was now where we were consuming it and eventually depositing it, albeit filtered through our teenage livers. It was a shrine to the circle of life for beer.

"Who needs a cigar?" Pat asked.

Each of us answered in turn and Pat passed them around. I lit mine using my candle flame and then hacked my rookie's cough. I was new to this vice and still unclear as to the attraction of the habit. To me, it was like smoke gargling. *You mean, you don't actually inhale, but just savor the introduction of toxins into your mouth?* I guess I didn't get it, but was willing to give it the old high school try, to be cool if for no other reason. After all, my father and grandfather both smoked cigars, so, heck, I was keeping a family tradition! The habit was undoubtedly part of the cause behind Grandpa Landwehr losing both of his legs because of blood clots, so I had that going for me. But he was old, and I was barely seventeen and invincible, so I puffed away like a caveman with a nic-fit.

With cigars lit, stinking up the limited oxygen in the place, Pete moved on to the next vice and popped the top off his beer using the church key, code words for the bottle opener. He passed the key around and we all did the same. Pete proposed a toast.

"To the caves!"

We raised our bottles and clinked them all around, saying, "To the caves!"

We all tilted our bottles and took swigs of the 3.2 carbonated disappointment. Being inside such an enormously natural formation suddenly gave validation to the dangerous entry we'd just undertaken, and it was cause for celebration. There in the dark, dank, fifty-five degree confines, us low lifes were living the high life.

Curious about the magnitude of the cave system, we took a look around. We relied on the small aura of light cast by our candles as we made our way from room to room. In the biggest room, a couple of guys stood around a small fire made of a twelve-pack container. These Rhode Scholars had determined that a small fire was more important than the precious oxygen the blaze was busy converting to carbon monoxide. We kept a distance from them as well as the rest of the folks we encountered. Most were other high schoolers looking for a thrill, but for some reason people kept to themselves in the darkness. It was some sort of cave etiquette. Party on, but keep your party over there, please.

Eventually we stopped exploring and formed a small circle. Now that we had seen the extent of the place, we were left with nothing to do but enjoy our vices. So we puffed away, and spat, and washed down the after-burn with a little beer. We talked about school and girls and music, and laughed riotously as we consumed the toxic stimulants of adulthood. The combination of adrenaline, alcohol and second-rate tobacco made everyone feel fine, even if a little dizzy. As the "straights" of Cretin High, we would never be as cool as the popular kids or the burnouts, but for now we had each other and we were as cool as we needed to be. So much of school was about fitting in and living up to the standards of others it was nice to be around friends who accepted you for who you were. Sure, we all had our little idiosyncrasies and annoyances, who doesn't? At the same time these guys were the best friends a kid my age could hope for. In this cave we had our own little Dead Poets' Society gathering, before it was even a thing.

An hour and a half later, our beers were gone, our candles were nearing the end of their useful lives and the novelty of the place had worn off. We figured we were fortunate to have made it this far, so the only thing remaining was to successfully exit via the little hobbit hole we'd come in through. We fumbled our way to the opening and, one by one, crawled into the dark, cylindrical abyss. Our trail of crawling teenage humanity was just as cramped as it was on the way in, but it was accompanied by outbursts of laughter as we cracked jokes along the way. A few cheap beers make every caver a comedian.

The caves expelled our carcasses into the cool evening air. *Air! Fresh air!* As good as it felt being inside our mysterious place, it felt redemptive to be outside again. The four of us stood and stretched. Collectively we'd entered the caves as boys and had come out as the same boys maybe a little stinkier and dirtier. But these caves were someplace we could assert our manhood with fire, alcohol, tobacco and bravado. It didn't make us any more adult to the rest of the world, but to us it was an emergence from the womb of our youth into the brink of what we thought it was to be a man.

***

Obsessed with our newly-discovered cavern of ill repute, we made a return trip a week later with the same cast of characters and the toxic ingredients of cheap cigars and beer. We made our way into the darkness with a tad more confidence and youthful certainty than the week before. I couldn't help but feel a mix of exhilaration and trepidation about returning. Part of me loved the element of risk in the experience, another part couldn't shake the feeling of uncertainty and fear the place held. This was a rock formation that had been around for hundreds of years so it was probably completely structurally sound and safe. But there was always that chance something could go wrong, someone could get hurt or we could somehow get trapped. None of this took into account the actual lawbreaking defiance of trespassing that underlay the whole adventure.

Once we'd wriggled our way in, we opened our beers and started exploring. After about an hour of roaming around drinking and smoking, we heard a guy from another group shout, "We are the Warriors!" At the time, *The Warriors* was a popular film and the phrase was one of the rallying cries of the movie. Doug didn't quite get the inference and countered with, "Well, we are the Raiders!" our school team name. Doug meant it in some sort of intended turf declaration response. Pat and I had a good chuckle at his reply. At the same time, we weren't looking for a fight, and something as mundane as a counter volley to the battle cry might just take us there.

A while later, I was standing in the dark, minding my own business, when suddenly I heard a bottle smash against the cave wall. I immediately felt a stinging sensation in my index finger.

"Hey, what the heck?" I shouted, moving the candle to look at my hand. Blood oozed from a half-inch cut on my index finger. I immediately stuck the finger in my mouth to clear the blood and assess the damage. As quickly as I cleared it, blood filled the slit. *What the heck?*

"My finger is cut!" I said. "Who smashed the bottle on the wall?" I asked of no one and everyone.

"What do you mean?" Pat asked.

I flashed the candle on the ground and saw the jagged edge of the bottle top laying in the sand. In a chance fluke, the shard cut me on its way to the floor. I put the finger in my mouth again and again to clear the blood, but it wasn't slowing. Doug handed me a clean tissue and I wrapped the wound as tightly as I could.

Dan and the rest of the guys gathered around.

"Guys, I hate to be a party pooper, but I might need stitches for this thing."

"Yeah, it's bleeding kinda bad," Pete added.

We'd seen pretty much all there was to see in our underworld, so made our way back to the entrance hole and, one by one, climbed our way up and out. I told Doug I wanted to stop at the SuperAmerica so I could get a package of Band Aids. He offered to give the rest of the guys a ride home while I conducted my gas station urgent care visit. We said our goodbyes and I got in the Volare' and made my way to West Seventh Street. I parked at SuperAmerica, went in and tried to look as casual as a teen could look buying Band Aids at 10:30 at night. The clerk gave me a side-eyed glance as I paid. I hurriedly grabbed the box and walked out the door. Back in the car, I opened the package and applied a couple of bandages to the finger. The bleeding seemed to have slowed, but the cut still looked deep enough to warrant concern.

How am I going to explain this one to Mom?

Yes, this would require the "good" son's best lie.

I got home, put on fresh Band Aids and went to bed. In the morning I approached Mom with the news. "Hey, Mom, Pete slammed my hand in a car door last night and cut it pretty good. I'm not sure if it needs stitches or not. What should I do?" I was not beyond throwing a friend under the bus for the chance at avoiding a good grounding or lecture. I'm sure Pete would be fine with taking one for the team.

"Let me take a look at it."

I peeled back the Band Aid and showed her the gash. The bleeding had subsided almost entirely, but the cut still looked deep.

"Hmmm, I don't know, hon. You might want to have that checked out with the doctor. Does it feel like any bones are broken?"

"No. Nothing hurts except the cut," I replied.

"Well, I have to be someplace. You know where the doctor's office is, right?"

"Yeah. Should I just drive myself?" I offered with the realization that if she said yes, it meant she was buying my lame attempt at an excuse for the wound.

"Sure. Just show them the insurance card, and it should all be covered."

"Okay. Thanks, Mom."

I took the Volare' down Lexington to the clinic about a mile away. After checking in, I was seated in an examination room. The doctor arrived a few minutes later and asked a few questions.

"So, you cut your finger. How did it happen?"

"Well, my buddy slammed it in a car door last night."

"Hmmm. Let's have a look," he said peeling back the bandage.

"Do you have any pain other than the cut? Maybe we should get an x-ray," he surmised.

"No, not really. None at all actually. Surprisingly, I guess." My thinly veneered lie was starting to make me dance around questions. I was never good at lying, but the circumstances surrounding this particular injury required it. Otherwise, I'd be exposed and my caving days would be over for good.

He went on to check it for strength and any signs of pain. I was stoic and non-reactive, so as to steer him away from any need for an x-ray. If there was one thing I was sure of, it was there were no broken bones to worry about.

"Well, from everything I can see, it's just a small cut. There don't appear to be any tendons cut and it's not terribly deep. Nothing a bandage shouldn't heal up in a few days," he said.

"So, no stitches?" I said, feigning concern despite my relief I'd be spared that experience.

"Nope. I'll have the nurse clean it up and you'll be on your way."

"That's great news. Thank you, Doctor," I said, in hopes my respect would help charm him into believing my lie.

I drove home feeling both relief and guilt. I'd dodged a bullet to be sure, but did it at the expense of my integrity. I was fortunate that in our family with six kids to worry about, Mom lived in a state of distracted vigilance. Between the demands of a big house, a full-time job, us kids and the stray pet of the month, she did kid triage as best she could. If we were not visibly limping or there were no protruding bones, we were left to lick our wounds, or take care of them. This time it meant sending me to the doctor alone. I was nearly eighteen and it was a sort of life skills test for me. I came away unscathed in the end and Mom was spared another divergence from what she planned to get done that day. She loved us, but she loved us more when we could take care of ourselves. It was a win-win, even if it did come with a small white lie attached.

***

In our search for new places of adventure, Pete heard of another set of caves on the opposite bank of the Mississippi River. Not only was it a new location, but someone said there was a dead horse that was supposed to be somewhere in the cave. No one seemed to know much about the horse or how it got there, let alone what a horse would be doing in a cave in the first place. Personally, I wondered if the smell alone wouldn't be enough to lead us right to it. But maybe not. Maybe the caves were at a temperature that preserved the horse enough to make decomposition slower. We just didn't know. These are the burning questions for a high schooler who would be better served focusing on his trigonometry. But they were questions that could only be answered by paying a visit. It seemed the place was just begging us to check it out. It must be done.

On Friday night, we gathered the usual suspects, drove over the Wabasha Street bridge and worked our way down to the river level.

We parked across the street and stealthed our way over to the cave entrance. The opening was much larger and more accessible than the ones across the river. We walked in barely needing to duck our heads to avoid the low ceiling. The caves had a different, less threatening feel to them. At the same time, they weren't as large or mysterious either. We poked around looking for signs of the dead horse. Because we were now seasoned cavers, we'd packed a couple of flashlights. Candles were okay, but flashlights give you more control and were more effective. In the main chamber, we flashed our beams around looking for, but not finding, any signs of the infamous dead horse.

"If there's a dead horse here, I don't smell it," I said as we wandered around the cavern.

"Me neither," Pat said.

"Holy crap, look at that!" Pete shined the light at the ceiling.

We craned our necks only to see a bat about a foot long hanging from the ceiling. It was black and brown with its wings wrapped tightly around its body. Now, there are a few things in life that make my skin crawl. Snakes for sure. Leeches and ticks, yep. But when it comes to the creep factor, bats take the cake. I know they get a bum rap. Sure, they eat hundreds of mosquitoes an hour, and have countless other benefits. But for me, they are Satan on the wing. Rabies in flight. Evil overhead. Blood sucking airborne rats. Death.

"Holy crap!" I said. "I don't like the looks of that."

"Me neither," Dan added.

"Well, I think I've seen enough," Pete said.

It was pretty clear I was not the only one with a dislike for the creatures. It is one thing to see a little four inch bat, but this one was over the limit. No one hesitated as we headed for the exit. The dead horse would have to wait for another night or perhaps another team of explorers, because we were having none of this winged mammal. We exited quickly and orderly so as to not rile it from its slumber.

I realize these juvenile ventures into the dark abyss were not among the greatest decisions in my young life. Tragedy lurked in the shadows the whole way, of that I am certain. But yet, we came away unharmed. At the time, I looked at it as pure adventure; teen energy and foolishness put in motion. We were pushing the envelope in our struggle for independence and on our road to adulthood. What else would explain drinking, smoking, using foul language and making other deviant choices? When I found out my own son was into "urban exploring," a modern-day equivalent where high schoolers explore abandoned or condemned buildings using headlamps and dark clothing, well, I guess I couldn't say much. About all I could do was warn him about the ramifications of getting caught. At the same time, there was a little part of me that wanted to buy a head lamp, fire up a stogie and join him.

***

Another of the big party spots of high school was "The Valley." I often overheard conversations from the cool kids about partying down in the Valley in nearby Highland Park. Being the straight kids we were never invited to such gatherings. So, on our own, we were determined to check out this whole Valley partying thing and maybe do a little ourselves.

Mike, a friend who was fairly new to our circle, was an intelligent, nice guy if a bit on the uptight side. He was also a high ranking officer in our JROTC program. Student officers at the time were held to a higher standard than the rank and file. We were expected to keep our noses clean and the higher your rank, the higher the standard set.

One Friday at school, Mike mentioned he managed to score a twelve pack of beer. He had some 'ski, as we referred to it. It was our teenage encrypted version of the word brewski to throw adults off our scent. We were ingenious that way, at least in our own minds. Because we were all underage, all we needed to find was a venue at which to drink Mike's acquired contraband. We agreed to meet that night and figure out the logistics on the fly.

Doug picked up Mike and then stopped by my house and got me. After that we swung around to Pete's place on Summit Avenue.

"Where should we go, guys? Got some brew to drink," Mike said.

"How about the Valley? Sometimes there are some good parties there," Pete replied.

"I've never been there, but what the hey, why not?" Doug chimed in.

Doug worked his way through the streets of Saint Paul as we rocked to Supertramp, Foreigner and Toto on the radio and jabbered about trigonometry, grades and sports. When we pulled into the lot of Valley Park, we were one of just a few cars. None of us were sure where to look for parties in the woods. Judging from the parking lot, it seemed the Valley was fairly desolate tonight. So, instead of wandering the woods, we broke out the beer and started drinking in the car. Because he was the driver, Doug opted out. He was content to just be part of the conversation. We were young and stupid, but we had moments of brilliance between us, and his choice to stay sober that night was one of them.

We sipped our beers and listened to the radio for about a half hour. As we finished each beer, we were careful to open our doors and put the empties underneath the car. No sense in getting caught with an open container when we finally hit the road. We were deep into our conversation as a car pulled into the dark parking lot and pulled behind us. The driver shut off his headlights, but left the parking lights on. We thought nothing of it and went back to drinking and talking smart.

A few minutes later, Doug said, "What is with this guy? Why is he leaving his parking lights on? It's so annoying." Mike and I craned our necks out the back window of the wagon to see who the offender was. It was then we saw the red and blue lights on top of the cruiser.

"Shit, man, it's a cop!" I said.

"For real?" Doug asked looking into the rearview mirror to get his own visual proof. He turned down the radio, because everyone knows cops hate music the most.

"Yep. Hide your beers, boys. Keep 'em low. Ugh, we're so busted," I said, setting my beer on the floor of the car.

"Holy shit, we've got all those cans sitting on the ground outside too. Like they're not going to see those," Pete said.

It was then the red and blue lights came on.

"Oh, man, there we go. Been nice knowing you guys. Be cool, everyone," Mike said.

"Yeah, be cool, be cool. Let Doug do the talking," I added.

"Hey, thanks a-hole. I'm not even drinking," Doug said.

The cop walked up to the driver's side window. "Evening gentlemen. Having a little party here?"

"Um, yeah. These guys are. I haven't had anything to drink tonight," Doug said, looking to throw us under the bus if that's what it took to get him off the hook.

"I see that. Can I see some identification from everyone?"

We all pulled out our driver's licenses and passed them to the officer. My heart thumped a thousand beats a minute at the thought I might be spending some time in jail. Hard time with a couple of other officers of Cretin. I was dying a slow death in the back seat. The thoughts ran through my head in rapid fire fashion.

We were just out to have a little fun, officer. Meant no harm.

Lord, if he lets us off, I promise I will never drink again.

Man, this tops anything my brother ever did at Cretin!

The cop returned to his squad car and ran our ID's. If we had one thing going for us, it was our clean records. It seems contradictory to say given our current predicament, but we really were good kids. We all had jobs, weren't into drugs and were respected in school. Heck, everyone in the car was an officer in Cretin's JROTC program. It was proof positive that even decent citizens mess up once in a while. My hope was the cop would recognize that for what it was and cut us a break.

"Man, we are so screwed," Mike said.

"Yeah, let's hope he's cool," Pete added.

Five minutes later, the cop sauntered up to Doug's window. "Okay, gentlemen, here's what I'm going to do. Because the driver appears to not be drinking, I'm going to let you dump the rest of those beers, then I want you to pick up these cans you've got outside here and vacate the premises. Is that understood?"

"Yes, sir. We appreciate that. Sorry for the trouble, officer," Doug said, using his best grovel.

"Yes, sir. Thank you, sir," the rest of us echoed like good cadets reacting to a higher ranking officer.

One by one, we got out of the car and started popping open cans of Miller High Life and dumping them on the ground. It was a bittersweet, yet redemptive moment. Part of it felt good, a washing away of our sins in puddles of fermented suds at our feet. We'd earned this punishment as part of our momentary pardon and, as penance, it was freeing. At the same time, dumping our hard-won, illegal brew on the ground almost brought a tear to my eye. This stuff was hard to come by and it seemed a sin to return it to the ground without it passing through our livers and kidneys first. But we poured them out anyway. It was a small price to pay for skirting a police record and we were happy to pay it. It was a different, more lenient time back then, for sure.

When we were done, the cop said, "Alright, gentlemen, you have a good evening, then."

"Will do. Thanks again," Doug said.

The cop returned to his cruiser, backed up and left the parking lot.

We climbed into the station wagon and each of us breathed a sigh of relief.

"Holy cow, that was close!" Pete said.

"No lie, man. We lucked out tonight!" I added.

"Yeah, that would have been bad, guys. Real bad," Mike said. As a car full of officers we were all grateful for the cop's mercy.

"Whew, the adrenaline rush. My heart is pounding. That sucked," Doug said.

I offered a suggestion, "What should we do now? How about getting pizza at Carbone's or something?"

"Yeah, that sounds good, actually," Doug agreed.

We drove to Carbone's and did what teens have done for generations. We hung out, ate pizza, drank Coca-Cola and talked. It was a stupid thing we'd done that night and we vowed each other to secrecy in the hopes our parents would never get wind of our brush up with the law.

These moments of situational stupidity were woven into our genetic code as teenagers in the seventies. We couldn't help ourselves. Our not-yet fully developed adolescent brains were taking us through life and we were just riding along without seatbelts. We were collectively weaving across four lanes of coming-of-age traffic like Ray Charles at the wheel, narrowly missing the ditch on the right and the median on the left. Sometimes, adolescence is all about cheating death and skirting the law. Thankfully, we all made it out alive and without the need for parole.

***

Once my friends and I reached our teen years, our need for wanderlust and travel seemed to get ratcheted up. Having our drivers' licenses and access to cars probably played a big part of it. Being away from home would also allow us to do what we wanted, when we wanted.

"I got permission from Grandma Grewe to use the cabin on Grand Lake if you guys want to go up for a night," Pete said.

"Really? Sweet! I'm in. I'll see if my brother Matt can come too," Pat replied.

"Yeah! I'm up for that. I can even drive my Cutlass, if needed," I added. I was proud to own my own vehicle, even if it was a liability on wheels. I had never taken it on a road trip before, but because Grand Lake was only an hour and a half away from St. Paul, it seemed like a manageable test for the car.

Pete's grandmother owned a cottage on the little lake in the middle of granite country in central Minnesota. My grandfather actually built a place on the same lake in the 1920's. The architecture of his cottage was strikingly unique because it was built with vertical logs instead of horizontal. It stood out among the rest of the horizontal log structures of the area. I'd visited the Landwehr cabin a handful of times as a kid and had great memories of the place. I never needed much excuse for a road trip, but knowing Grandpa's place was on the same lake as the Grewe cabin made Pete's offer even more justifiable.

The four of us made plans to go up on a weekday afternoon in August. Matt was a couple of years younger than the rest of us and had football camp the following day, so the plan was to stay for only one night. School for all of us started in a couple of weeks, so we thought it would be a good chance to get out of the Twin Cities and blow off a little steam. One last blast of summer vacation before our fall term began.

We piled into the green machine and headed out to the interstate. After a twenty minute ride, we switched over to Highway 10, a four-lane stretch of highway memories for me. I'd taken many trips on it as a kid on visits to Saint Cloud to see Dad's side of the family. Most of those rides were wrought with one or another carsick sibling, depending on who was relegated to the back seat. With six of us, it seemed there was always someone vomiting into a McDonald's bag after succumbing to the throes of motion sickness. As my friends and I chugged on down the highway, I thought about my poor mom and was grateful that carsickness was a thing of the past and this trip would have none of that.

"Just wait, guys. A few more weeks and it'll be back to shining shoes and polishing brass," I said.

"Yeah, don't remind me," Pat said. While most of us didn't mind high school, Pat in particular was never a big fan of the whole experience. In his upper class years at Cretin, he was working a lot of late nights at the Lexington, and, over time, it took a toll on his applying himself. Eventually it crept into his attitude, as well. Like many people, Pat would argue high school wasn't his favorite phase of life.

The Oldsmobile hummed along with its big gas guzzling 350 engine as we listened to the AM radio. We passed through Saint Cloud and then worked our way northwest. Once we started seeing granite monuments and quarries, I knew we were getting close. The region was an area rich in the rock, and the source of the nearby town of Rockville's name.

When we pulled into Rockville, Pat said, "Maybe we can get some beer here."

"That sounds like a great idea," I added, never one to dismiss a good one, especially if it didn't involve me. Matt and I were the youngest and looked the part. This exempted us from being the ones who would be making the attempt at an illegal purchase.

Pete asked, "Who's going to try and get it?"

I laughed and said, "Well, you've always had the best success, Pete."

"Maybe that's because I'm the only one who ever tries," he added.

"I can't help my baby face," I said. Truth was, I was a bit terrified at the thought of trying to falsify my identity in any way. I was a rule follower through and through. Except for the actual underage drinking part of the equation, of course.

Pete relented and went into the liquor store. The three of us sat in the car, silently hoping for a small, carbonated miracle. Ten minutes later, Pete and a clerk came out carrying two cases of beer, Special Export and Cold Spring. While we were overjoyed he came out with anything, the net take was a mixed blessing. Special Export was a beer brewed in La Crosse, Wisconsin by Heileman Brewing. Their trademark green bottle was the agent behind a carbonated, skunky, not-quite-right flavor. Its secret ingredient made you wish you were dead the morning after drinking. I know it did for me on more than one occasion. The beer aptly earned its name as the "Green Death." It was a moniker that made its appeal even more suspect.

Perhaps worse, was the other beer, Cold Spring. It was the wildcard, a beer none of us had ever tried. A local beer brewed in the next town over from Rockville. Pete chose it because it was cheap. We were all on budgets, so cheap worked for us. Soon enough, we would all discover exactly why cheap did not equate with enjoyable or good. For the moment though, we let the realization that we were forty-eight beers richer sink in. It was a momentary victory in Rockville.

When Pete got to the car, I popped the trunk and he and the clerk loaded the cases. Then, Pete put a few of each kind into a cooler of ice. He jumped in the passenger seat and we all whooped. "Score!" Pat proclaimed. Score indeed. The stage was set for a wild day at the lake.

We drove through Rockville in the dog days heat of August. My sinuses were thick and my eyes itched with hay fever that was having its way with me. It was always in its full glory this time of year. I'd forgotten my antihistamines back home, so was forced to tough it out and make the best of a bad deal. I was on vacation, after all, and maybe a couple of beers would help take the edge off.

The dust billowed up behind our car as we transitioned from pavement to dirt roads. After a few minutes, I pulled the car into Grandma Grewe's driveway. Everyone piled out of the two-door Oldsmobile and headed in to check out our digs for the night. The northern air wafted of lake water and pines and gave me an immediate sense of comfort and relaxation. When we walked in the distinct cabin smell embraced us. The scent was a soothing mix of old books, and coffee and fireplace smoke from fires of the past. Ah, it was going to be a fun day.

Everyone grabbed their stuff, picked out beds for the night and rolled out their sleeping bags. We took a walk around and checked out the cabin for a bit. It had that old cabin charm with a quilt over the couch, a nice rocking chair and old, but not-quite-antique lamps. Scattered around the room on shelves and end tables were books, puzzles and old magazines available for those rainy days. Personally, it wasn't quite as charming as Grandpa Landwehr's cottage, but it had its own quaintness to it.

When we went out to the yard, we were ecstatic to find horseshoe pits. This was a game Pat had taken to recently, and his zeal for playing was contagious, so we'd all become regular players. None of us were as good as Pat, but we were willing to entertain his obsession with chucking the irons.

"Hey, horseshoes anyone?" Pat asked.

"Yeah, but first things first. Anyone need a brew?" I answered, heading for the kitchen.

Pete and Matt concurred and followed me back into the cabin. Pat said he was on the wagon. Something in the recent past had caused him to quit drinking for a time. I was a little sorry to see he was taking a break on this trip, but had to honor it as a noble decision. It was always better to have all my friends on board when I was looking to go on a bit of a tear, and to have my partner in crime sitting this one out didn't feel right. Nevertheless, I grabbed a Cold Spring and Pete and Matt each chose a bottle of the Green Death. Being the wisest of all of us, Pat grabbed a Sprite, mostly to have something to do with his hands while the rest of us drank our beers. When everyone was set, we ambled back to the horseshoe pit area.

"Who's got the church key?" I asked.

Pete passed the bottle opener to me. Even though we were all underage at the time, we'd perfected the lingo that goes with a good bout of drinking.

"A toast to the cabin!" Pete said.

"To the cabin, and to Pete for scoring the beer," I added.

We all clinked our bottles together and took a celebratory swig. For the moment we were lake home owners, if only for one night, and the feeling was one of complete freedom.

The humid air brought a quick sweat to the bottles we drank from. The Cold Spring had a sharp, biting flavor unlike any I'd ever experienced, and not in a good way. It changed character three times before hitting my stomach, from the first refreshing sip, to a rotgut middle and a strange, tangy kick at the end.

"Well, that's an interesting beer, eh?" I said.

"Let me try a sip," Pat said. He momentarily stepped out of his weekend abstinence and took a swig to see what the hubbub was about.

"Yeah, weird tasting. Not exactly the champagne of beers," he said in reference to our favorite brand, Miller High Life.

"To me it's like a fricken' buffet. The flavor just keeps changing as it goes down. Not entirely good, but, hey, it's beer!" I said.

"Here's to beer! Let's throw some shoes," Matt said, raising his bottle of Green Death.

We all took another swig and broke up into teams. Horseshoes is one of those sports where you can drink beer the whole time with little impact on your overall performance. In fact, I would venture to say beer drinking while playing horseshoes is almost recommended. This was an alcoholic's advantage we exercised on this occasion when we actually had some beer. Channeling our inner hick, we flung the iron shoes back and forth. For a bunch of young city boys, we were pretty accomplished players, so the games didn't take long.

Despite their unappetizing taste, the beers went down quickly for the first part of the afternoon. Pat put Jackson Browne's, *Running on Empty* album into the cassette player and cranked it up. If there was an LP soundtrack for the relationship between Pat, Pete and myself, that was it. Over our high school years, we'd taken to it and it became an album full of anthems for us. It spoke of life as a young rock star on the road and all that goes with it. It was required listening for every road trip and resonated deeply with each of us.

By late afternoon, everyone was feeling good. Our laughter rolled across the lake as we recounted funny stories from high school and our families. At one point, someone slung a horseshoe, and it landed oddly, bounced and took on a roll that caused the guys on the opposite side to scatter for fear of it rolling into their shin. It careened toward a half-full beer and smashed it like a bowling headpin. All four of us doubled over in laughter. Beer has chemical magic to make incredibly unfunny things seem like a complete scream and, at the moment, we were witnessing one.

"So much for getting our deposit back on *that* case of bottles," I said.

This triggered more unfounded riotous laughter among the four of us. It was the funniest broken bottle in all of our lives, that much was sure. We were drunk monkeys.

After a few more games, the novelty of horseshoes and crappy beer wore off. We wandered back to the cabin. Matt said, "I'm going to take a row in the boat if that's okay, Pete?"

"Sure thing," Pete answered.

While he was on the water, we snacked on chips for a bit and lazed around the cabin. After a good beer buzz on a warm afternoon, we resorted to naps or down time reading magazines.

An hour later, Pat started to get concerned. "I wonder where Matt is. He's been gone a while and he was pretty buzzed." In a show of well-founded concern, he headed out the door of the cabin to scan the lake for his brother. After a few more anxious moments, he spotted a rowboat making a course in the direction of our dock.

"I think that's him out there, headed this way."

Ten minutes later, Matt walked onto shore from the dock. Pat greeted him.

"Where were you, man? I was worried sick, brother."

"Sorry, Pat. I was rowing off my buzz. That Green Death, man," Matt said apologetically.

Pat laughed and said, "No problem. I'm just glad you're okay."

Meanwhile, I was fighting my own battle. The bad beer buzz combined with my hay fever allergies was kicking my butt. I was stuffed up and my eyes were scratchy. It appeared this day-drinking event during the dog days of August was proving to be a bust. Here we were, trying to live the life of rock stars without the long hair, recklessness or stamina. Or, maybe the whole drinking thing was overrated. It was hard to tell from behind the fog of my hay fever and a looming Cold Spring hangover.

The rest of the evening continued to coast on a road of aimlessness. We were all done with the drinking thing, due in no small part to the quality of the beer we chose. It was becoming clear we peaked too early. Or maybe we just got the nonsense out of the way right at the start. After talking over our options on how to finish out the day, we drove to a drive-in theater in hopes of seeing a decent movie. When we got there all that was showing was some G-rated movie that didn't look appealing to any of us.

During the ride back to the cabin we tuned into the Doctor Demento radio show. The program featured goofy songs and comedy bits played over the air by the crazy host, Doctor Demento. We laughed at the variety of songs and even sang along when we knew the words. The show was light and entertaining, so much so we tuned it in when we got back to the cabin. We played cards and snacked for a bit as we listened to the doctor play goofy songs like, "10,000 Pounds of Bananas" and, "Put the Lime in the Coconut."

This cabin time was simple, wholesome fun at the end of a long day. There was no pressure to drink and get crazy. When it came right down to it, winding down easy came at a cost significantly less than a debilitating Green Death hangover. We started the day as adults and were seemingly ending it in our more familiar, sensible places as teenagers. While we were stretching our wings, it was clear we were not quite ready for all that comes with adulthood. It was also a reminder that while being an adult was something we were careening into, our journey didn't preclude us from having fun as kids, singing songs about 10,000 pounds of bananas.

CHAPTER 16: CARS

There comes a time in every teen's life where they want their own car. It typically happens immediately after they pass their driver's test. At that age, a car signifies boundless freedom. All rational thought takes a back seat to the allure of four wheels and the open road. Now that I had my license, I wanted my own car, badly. Granted, my siblings and I all had access to Mom's Volare', a car which was the antithesis of cool. But when you are timesharing a car between two other siblings and your mom, it gets kind of annoying. It was always spoken for when I wanted it most, so I was routinely left to rely on a friend to cart me around.

I started asking around work to see if anyone knew where I could get a reliable used vehicle for cheap. I was yet to learn that reliable and cheap are conflicting terms in the automotive world. I was obsessed with the thoughts of freedom that owning my own vehicle promised. Like most kids, I had dreams of taking off in my reliable, cheap used car for California, or some other distant destination. Such is the mind of a newly-licensed adolescent driver.

I was not alone in my desires for free access to a vehicle. My friend Pete got bit by the used car trap in a big way. He bought a late '60s Chevy Impala for one hundred dollars from the night shift head dishwasher at the Lexington Restaurant. The car was a maroon colored rust bucket that was jacked-up in the back, giving it a cool, gear head look. It came complete with over 100,000 miles on the odometer and, for no extra charge, a high-pitched squealing front tire that left a skid mark wherever it went. This bonus feature meant Pete need never give notice if he was picking any of us up, as we would be able to hear him coming from two blocks away. It served as a sort of poor man's car alarm. If it was ever stolen, one could just follow the skid marks and listen for the squealing.

I remember being both jealous of and shocked by Pete's purchase. After all, it did move, it had seats, an engine and, with the help of a body shop and a personal mechanic, a small stitch of potential. Pete was soon to find out it should have had a dollar bill slot next to the ignition that accepted only denominations featuring Andrew Jackson. It was to serve as Pete's first exposure to a money toilet.

None of us friends could deny that the jacked-up back end of the Impala was ultra-cool, because it was. But when the rubber hit the road, and, in this case, stayed there, the greaser-mobile lost some coolness. You could barely hear the radio over the squealing tires. It was more than the back end of this car that was jacked-up. The whole car was. As in, jacked-up, jacked-up!

Don, the guy that sold Pete the car, told him the reason for the noise and tire issue was a bent tie rod and the repair would cost about $150.00. Pete thought nothing of it because Don gave him such a deal on the hundred dollar price tag. When Pete took the vehicle in to get the tie rod fixed, the garage told him it was not a tie rod, but rather a bent axle and repairs would cost him over five hundred dollars. So, instead of fixing it, the car sat in Pete's driveway, serving as a large snowdrift over the winter. During his ownership, Pete only drove it a few times, though he did occasionally sit in it and listen to the radio. If nothing else, it was his own personal hundred dollar stereo. Eventually, his father tired of it sitting in his driveway and told him he had to get rid of it. Pete ended up junking it and getting twenty-five dollars for it from a salvage company.

Jealous of Pete's incredible deal, I found out about a "good deal" of my own. It was offered by another employee of the Lexington, Anne, a waitress who was looking to offload her '68 Oldsmobile Cutlass in the summer of 1978. She might have mentioned it had over 100,000 miles on it, but I was pretty much tone deaf after she said she'd part with it for a paltry three hundred dollars. Sometimes we hear what we want to hear. Money does strange things to a teen's sensibilities.

When I mentioned the idea to my sister Jane, she wanted in on this seemingly incredible deal, almost sight unseen. The thought of having an investment partner in the sale made it seem even more affordable for me. Neither of us had a firm grasp on the financial implications of owning a vehicle, but how hard could it be, really? A little gas, a little oil, a tune up here, a two dollar wash there. Nothing to it.

I set up a time with Anne to go and take a look at it. I showed up to her apartment and she took me out to the car. It was a low-slung beast with a hunter green paint job. I walked up to take a closer look.

On the driver's side, the door molding was missing. Hubcaps were missing all around, the vinyl roof had a small tear in it and there were pockets of rust near the rear wheel wells. The plastic grill in front was missing a small section and even though we were looking at it in the middle of summer, the car was equipped with snow tires in the back. Retreads, no less.

The whole vehicle was a vision of unparalleled, exquisite beauty.

I walked around the car, kicked the tires a bit and asked Anne if I could take a look at the engine. She obliged and popped the hood open. I took a peek at the big V8, 350 cubic inch engine as if I knew what I was looking for. *Look, there's the air cleaner. Yep, and there's some spark plug wires. Oh, and this is where you put the oil. Yep, looks good to me!*

It was then she said, "Turns out I've got another guy interested who said he'd give me $400.00. I told him I already had a prospect, so if you still want it Jim, you can have it for $400.00 instead of $300.00. Does that sound okay?"

My anxiety jumped. Suddenly I was in a bidding war, even if it was just a seller's charade, which I'm fairly certain it was. The thought of someone else getting this jewel clouded my better judgement.

"Uh, yeah. I'll have to check with my sister on that, but it shouldn't be too much of a problem," I replied. I was a car dealer's dream. *Of course, you're going to want the rustproofing with that, right?*

She gave me the keys and I climbed into the cracked vinyl driver's seat to see how I liked the feel of it. The interior smelled a bit girlish for my liking, but was nothing that couldn't be overcome with a good pine tree air freshener hanging from the cigarette lighter when this mean machine was all mine. I noted the radio was AM only, a problem I would have to address, as all the good stations were on the FM band. Again, not a deal breaker, just an inconvenience.

"Could I take a test drive to show it to my sister? I live a couple miles from here," I said.

"Sure thing. I'll see you in a little bit," Anne answered.

I turned the key and after a couple seconds of cranking, the car fired up. I put it into gear and pulled away slowly. I worked my way over to Summit Avenue, which would allow me to open it up a bit. The speed limit was only thirty miles per hour, but I was just looking to test the acceleration. A few blocks into my cruise down Summit, I punched the gas pedal down to the floor. The car hesitated for a second before it kicked in and pressed my back into the seat. I attributed the slight hesitation to the need for a tune-up, dirty plugs or something of the sort, it was just a guess. Ultimately, once the horsepower kicked in, it impressed me enough to be convinced this was the car for me.

Once I was assured the car had the proper torque, I backed my speed down to five over the limit. I turned on the AM radio and because the car was missing its antenna, I struggled to pull in a station. I already knew the radio was going be an issue, and this just confirmed the fact. It was a small inconvenience among many other small inconveniences I could surely overlook given the prospect of co-owning my own car.

When I got home, I parked and went in to get Jane. She came out and gave the Oldsmobile a once over. She wasn't much for details like the engine and the miles so much as the "cool factor." Fashion over function. As cars go, there were a lot less cool vehicles than the Cutlass. Take the Volare', for example. Take it please! As it turned out, later in life Jane would upgrade to a Chevy Camaro, the quintessential cool car, albeit a bit of a mechanical lemon. But, for now, she was willing to settle for the geriatric Cutlass. The car wore cool like a sixty year-old in bell bottoms.

"Well, I guess it'll work," Jane said with tempered enthusiasm.

"Yeah? Oh, and she wants four hundred for it now, as it turns out. Says there's another interested buyer. I know it's more than what we expected, but we should probably jump if we want it."

"Well, that sucks. But I suppose…" she said.

"Cool. I still think it's not a bad deal, despite the increase. I'll go tell her we're interested."

I got behind the wheel and headed back to Anne's. When I arrived I told her we would take it and that I'd bring the money later that week.

***

Early into my ownership of our "new" ten year-old car I began to uncover a few of its shortcomings, some of which came at a higher cost than others. The first order of business was to make the interior look a little better. I went to the local auto parts store and bought the cheapest seat cover I could to hide the cracked front vinyl seats. The cover was made out of stretchy nylon and elastic. After pulling all of its tethering straps tight, the bench seat took on that almost new look. The cover actually hid a number of highly visible sins. Unfortunately, within two weeks of buying it, a snag developed and became a run that ran vertically up the nylon cover, returning the front seat to the character it once had. Namely, torn.

The vehicle had what I like to call "steering slop." When you turned it, there was always a slight delay before something actually happened. Or, when cruising down the road, you could jiggle the steering wheel a little left or right without affecting the actual direction the car was travelling. The steering wheel swayed left and right with no effect. I assumed it was just in need of a front end alignment, so took it to a garage to have it looked at. The mechanic told me the linkages were worn on the entire front end. The whole repair job would cost hundreds of dollars, not the seventy dollars I'd hoped for. For that cost, I could learn to live with a little slop.

Over time, the Cutlass developed a series of interior glitches I came to tolerate. One of them was the headlight switch that came off in my hand one day. A piece of plastic broke off and, after checking with the auto parts store, I was told it would be an expensive thing to replace. At this point in my life, anything over twenty dollars was expensive, so it seemed the cheap fix was to let the light switch dangle from the connecting wires under the dash, near my left foot. It was low class, but as long as the lights came on when I pulled out the knob-less lever, I didn't much care what people thought.

Another annoyance was the floating gas gauge. When I gunned the engine, the needle visibly dropped a little, only to float back up. We never really knew what this meant when we were near an empty tank, so Jane and I were careful to buy three dollars' worth when things got dicey. I don't recall the gauge ever being much above the half tank notch anyway, but that was not the fault of the car. It was more because of the skinflints behind the wheel.

As I mentioned, the radio never really worked well at all. We would have invested in a car stereo if we thought the car was worth it. I never realized how much I missed a car radio until I didn't have one. I tried using a pop-up cassette recorder propped on the seat next to me for a while. The sound was ridiculously tinny. After a few uses, the process of bringing it along every trip then hiding it under the seats at every destination made it far more work than it was worth. Instead I learned to listen to the hum of the engine as it shifted through the gears.

And then there was the heater. It worked pretty well except when the fan was turned to the highest setting, when it shut off altogether.

This technical glitch was again estimated to be in the hundreds of dollars. Broke as usual, I turned to a low cost fix to the problem called the "medium setting fix." Who needs a high fan speed on their heater during a Minnesota winter anyway? Such luxuries.

To add to the matter, the rear window had a tendency to frost up in the winter, especially if there was more than one person in the car. I took the situation into control by equipping the passenger in the back seat with my scraper. When things got too frosty, they were required to scrape the inside of the window so I could see out the back. Eventually, I got wise and purchased a plastic frost-free window porthole at 10,000 Auto Parts. It was an oval shaped piece of plastic that adhered to the window, creating an airspace that always stayed clear. It was a perfect solution until it developed a crack that defeated the whole concept. Sometimes it's hard to have nice things. I eventually tore it off and kept the scraper at the ready. The manual method would have to serve.

***

The Cutlass' reputation for disappointment continued to bleed me dry financially. In the early fall, true to form, the car developed a ticking noise. Based on my initial poor assessment of the front end alignment, I decided to enlist the help of my brother Tom in troubleshooting the noise. We popped the hood and took a look. It didn't take him long to say, "It sounds like your alternator has a bad bearing."

"Any idea what that is going to cost me?"

"Well, if I were you, I'd do it myself. You can get a used one at a junkyard for cheap and put it in yourself."

Now, the only thing more lacking than my mechanical aptitude is my confidence in my mechanical aptitude. At the same time, I am the world's most frugal person, so I decided to take the job on myself when the voltage light on the car began to flicker a few weeks later. I went to the junkyard, bought a used alternator for eighty dollars and installed it in a couple of hours accompanied by a colorful tapestry of curse words and a couple of skinned knuckles. It was a confidence booster that made me think maybe this car maintenance thing wasn't as hard as people made it out to be.

Over time, the battle between me and Jane for control of the car became more than I wanted to deal with. As teens, we were both always on the run, and trying to schedule who got the car and when, especially on the weekends, became a big hassle. I saved my money and eventually I paid her back the two hundred dollar initial investment. Looking back, this buy-out payment decision thereby putting all the repair costs solely upon my back, sums up my investment savvy. My savvy also explains why I didn't make my first million by the age of thirty.

Winter brought its own bag of problems for my beloved Oldsmobile. In the bitter cold of a Minnesota January, the Cutlass was difficult to start. The big V8 engine took a lot of amperage to crank, so when the air temps were extreme, extended grinding on the poor starter took a toll on the battery. If I pumped the gas pedal too much in frustration, the engine flooded and there was nothing I could do but wait it out for a few cold minutes while it dried. Eventually, after having the battery die in a couple of different instances, I got a feel for whether there was any chance she would turn over, or if continuing to crank it was just a waste of time. You sort of develop a relationship with a car that way.

When I went looking for advice, Tom told me that maybe I should try using starter fluid. He said it worked wonders for his car on occasion. "What is starter fluid?" I asked.

"It's sort of like spraying jet fuel into your carburetor. It's probably not good to use it a lot, but it really helps cold weather starts."

Well, that was all I needed to hear. Later that week I went to our local 10,000 Auto Parts store and bought a can. The next time the temperature was below zero, I went out to the green beast and tried to start it. I ground the starter in futility. So, I moved on to Plan B. I got the can of starting fluid out of the trunk, took off my mittens and sprayed a good shot of it into the long tubular opening of the air cleaner. I climbed behind the wheel, turned the key and the car fired up instantly. *That stuff is miraculous!* I was shocked at how easy it made an otherwise stressful event. Why didn't everyone use this stuff all the time?

My answer came during follow-up episodes. Over time, the car became more and more dependent on the starting fluid at seemingly warmer temperatures than in the past. It was like a drug addict who needs increasingly larger doses of the drug to attain the level of high that used to come from lower doses. My car was a starting fluid junkie! Or, perhaps I just grew impatient with messing around with all the usual unsuccessful gyrations and went straight for the quick hitter. In any case, when combined with another brutal Minnesota winter, it was the beginning of the end for her.

***

Early in January of 1979, the Lexington restaurant staff held a Christmas party and dinner at a restaurant in Highland Park. I picked up my friend and fellow busboy Tim Ivory at his house and we made our way to the restaurant. We laughed with our coworkers and enjoyed a dinner of prime rib, baked potato and salad. It was a great night where having my own car and acting all adult-like felt pretty good.

At the end of the evening, we went out to the Cutlass and I turned the key. The starter grinded away for ten seconds before I turned the key back. I tried again for another seven second crank with the same result.

"Hmmm," I said, turning to Tim.

"Does it do this a lot?" Tim asked.

"Not really. This is a new thing. Not a good new thing, mind you. But a new thing."

I tried a third time and after a few seconds she coughed and turned over.

"Never fear!" I said fearfully.

I put it in gear and pulled out of the parking lot. We cruised down to Cleveland Avenue and took a right. About halfway down the block, the car sputtered and died.

"What the...?" I said.

"Uh-oh. Is this another new thing?" Tim asked.

"Um, yeah it is."

I switched on the flashers and coasted to the side of the road. I had no starting fluid in the car, and I had no plan B, so we sat in the cold for thirty seconds or so before I turned the key again. The car sputtered and hacked like an old man, but died immediately after starting. Fearing I would flood the engine, I let it sit for a minute, thinking my patience would grant me a little mercy from God above.

I tried it again and she fired up. I revved the engine hard, repeatedly. This is an old trick from way back and has been known to fix a litany of nagging automotive issues. If nothing else, it gives the driver a sense of power over an incalcitrant vehicle. After a few good revs, I put it in drive and we proceeded on down the roadway.

A quarter mile down the road, the car chugged and wheezed and died again. I pulled over, put on the flashers again and let it sit for a minute.

"This doesn't look so good does it?" Tim said with a degree of concern.

"No, it doesn't."

I turned the key and the starter screeched reluctantly for fifteen seconds or so before it finally started. The engine ran for a couple of seconds and then died again.

"What the…? Aw, c'mon Bessie, don't do this to me!" I pleaded.

I cranked for another extended period before the engine finally turned over. This time I revved it hard again before shifting into gear and pulling into the lane. I sped up Cleveland Avenue and took a right onto Summit. I made it a block up Summit before the car died again. This ridiculous routine continued on for another two blocks. Crank, start, rev, drive, die, repeat. By the third block of Summit Avenue, the battery reached the end of its life. When I turned the key, it just clicked.

"I don't like the sound of that," Tim said.

"The sound of death."

Suddenly having my own car and all the adult-like responsibility that comes with it felt pretty heavy and overrated.

"I think they call this dead in the water," he said.

"Yep, I'll head to the gas station over there and call home, I guess."

I got out into the cold January night, walked a block over to Grand Avenue and called my brother Tom from the pay phone in the station. About twenty minutes later, he showed up in Mom's car with some jumper cables. He hooked them up and we managed to get the battery charged. Tom switched cars with Tim and me. He fired up the car and after a half dozen more short two or three block driving stints followed by some long-grinding starts, he succeeded in limping the car to the street in front of our house. Tom got out, walked up to me and Tim in Mom's car.

"It seems to be firing okay when it's running, but it just keeps getting fuel starved. I can't say for sure, but I think it might be your fuel filter," he said.

"Huh. Is that something I could do myself?"

"Oh yeah. Shouldn't be too tough."

My brother neglected to say it shouldn't be too tough for a confident, qualified mechanic with the right tools for the job in a heated garage.

I took Tim home and apologized for the inconvenience my heap of junk had caused him. He understood and wished me good luck.

Determined to save myself a few bucks, I committed to fixing the car later in the week after I assessed the job and bought the parts. To my chagrin, when I came out to the car the next day, the back driver's side tire was flat. Such is the dependability of a well-worn retread snow tire in cold weather. It seemed like it was one thing after another with this "ticket to freedom" I'd spent so much hard-earned money on.

Snow was in the forecast, and I knew the vehicle would have to be moved off the street for plowing. Cars parked on the wrong side of the street during a plow event were ticketed, and I didn't need that added aggravation. I went into the cold street, jacked up the vehicle, removed the flat retread and replaced it with an even sketchier spare tire, a summer tread at that. Once the tire was changed, I started the car and limped it across the street to the Saint Luke's Church parking lot, a gathering place for the neighborhood cars during plowing season.

A couple days later, I packed up my tools and headed over to the lot. I popped the hood and set to work on removing the fuel filter. As I understood it, the filter was made of paper and located in a metallic housing along the fuel line. I located it, sized my crescent wrench to it and started a counter clockwise turn to loosen the filter's housing. After a turn or two, I realized the fuel line was also twisting, thereby pinching the fuel flow. Worried I might be ruining the line, I panicked and cranked the fuel filter housing clockwise again back to its original tightness.

I stepped back and assessed my predicament. It appeared the coupler the housing was threaded into should not turn, but the dang thing was torqued so tight, nothing but a good grunting would loosen it. Determined to dominate the task and force the vehicle to submit to my mechanical Lordship, I wrenched it again, this time trying to prevent the line from turning with the housing. Again the metal line pinched nearly closed.

"Argh! What the heck, man?" I shouted. Was there no end to the frustration of owning this cursed green hulking hunk of rusting, decrepit, undependable, money-sucking scrap metal?

It was the winter of my discontent.

At this point, my rage was blended with equal parts determination and stubbornness to cloud any clarity of thought. I was in deep and saw no way out but to go for broke. So I cranked the wrench back clockwise, tightening the whole assembly to try again from the start. As I cranked it with gentle force, the line again twisted and a hairline split revealed itself, the result of too much back and forth twisting.

"Mother of Mary, Jesus and Josephine!" I shouted into the frosty Minnesota air. My words hung in the vapor. I raged and fumed for a few minutes in absolute disbelief at the incredible streak of bad luck I seemed to be having, much of it by my own hand. I'd essentially cut a hole in the jugular vein of my car's fuel system. It was human-assisted automotive suicide. I had no idea what it would cost to replace a split fuel line, but gauging from the deep dark places the tubing snaked down to, my guess was A LOT.

Then and there, in that cold, desolate parking lot, my affection for the freedoms afforded by car ownership gave way to defeat. The car had beaten me into submission. I no longer loved her. Over the course of our short life together, she'd done nothing but take, take, take. Our love affair was a one-way street. We'd come to a dead end. It wasn't me, it was her. Definitely her.

I was done.

Within a week, I called a junk dealer, who arranged to haul the car away for fifty dollars. On the bright side, it was twice the amount Pete got for his junker. He arranged to tow it from the lot a few days later. When he showed up, I gave the guy my title and took his check. The car was the worst investment of my short life, but I was determined to move on.

My struggles with her continued, however. A few months after I sold it, my sister Jane started receiving notices from the City of Minneapolis threatening her with a court appearance if she didn't pay parking tickets issued to the car, which neither of us any longer owned. It turns out the junk dealer replaced the engine of my car and neglected to transfer the title or change the plates. The guy had parking issues too, evidently. A shyster at multiple levels.

Because the title was still in Jane's name, she had to go to the City and contest that we sold the vehicle months prior. Eventually, after enough pleading and paperwork, she was cleared of the tickets and the guy was put on notice he needed to transfer the title. It was the perfect bad ending to the perfect bad investment.

While this car was nothing but a bucket of problems, it taught me some important lessons about the cost of ownership. I quickly discovered there is no end to the money you can dump into a vehicle. The price for the freedom of the open road is rich, one no teenager should be chained to. At the same time, I suspect my teenage first car experience is a universal one. If teens could afford newer, well-running vehicles, they would. Instead they have to settle for the has-beens, the castoffs, the uglies and the beaters. My car fit all of these descriptors and it came to me having been ridden hard and put out to my gullible teenage pasture. It was good to finally be free from it.

***

Perhaps the coolest car of my days at Cretin was Pete's Cadillac. I should clarify, it was his dad's Cadillac convertible. His daddy's Caddy, I guess you could say. Like an aircraft carrier on wheels, it was a monstrously large 1970 Coupe Deville with a baby blue paint job and a luxurious white leather interior. It was a two-door model, which made the doors long and heavy, given the length of the car. When you slammed them it was thunderous, like the door to a bank vault. The radial tires had wide whitewalls making the ride gloriously smooth. To add to its appeal, the convertible roof was mechanically driven and magically retracted itself with the push of a button once the metal releases were let in front. Convertibles were sort of ridiculous in a state where they could only be used for three months a year, at best. But on those warm days with the top down, there was nothing better.

On the inside, the car was all about the details. The radio knobs and heating and cooling controls gleamed with a chrome finish. The door arm rests had long control panels with electric locks and windows, luxuries my mom always found as excessive and unnecessary in her car purchases. "They just drain your battery, and what happens when they break? Big money!" she'd say. Despite her sensibilities, I thought power windows were the best invention ever, as did every other kid who ever played with them.

Of course, the car was equipped with a host of other niceties the common, working-class folk couldn't afford. Little things like power seats, air conditioning, and, best of all, an eight track player with a large single "stereo" speaker in the back and two in the front. The rear speaker was built right into the center of the seat at head level. The location of it made any thought at all of participating in conversation with anyone in the front seat a laughable impossibility. Back there, you were in an audiological dead zone, an echo chamber of yourself. At the same time, I always thought it was a novel design, as most cars had them set into the back platform under the rear window. Where this one was positioned gave the Caddy character.

Pete's father had an aftermarket old-timey "Ahhoogah" horn added to the car. It was triggered by a button below the dash, and Pete used it with regularity. When he sounded its trademark "Ahhoogah" it was my alert he was outside my door waiting to take us somewhere. He was known to use it to attract attention from girls around Derham Hall on occasion as well, as if a long blue Cadillac convertible driven by a teenage boy didn't attract attention enough.

Pete's father was a successful attorney and this car was technically his wife's. He had a newer, more luxurious Eldorado that was off limits to Pete for the most part. So we slummed around in his Coupe Deville instead. Believe me, coming from a single-parent family of six kids, I knew what a privilege it was to be escorted around in such an opulent vehicle. It sort of fell under my own self-penned "philosophy of want" which goes, *I will probably never own a cabin by a lake, but it's sure nice to have friends who do.* The same philosophy held true as a teen with a friend who had access to a Cadillac.

The car took us everywhere. We went to Twins games, took it to school, proms and Friday night football games. While the thought of the Caddy's kickin' stereo held great allure for Pat, Dan and I as rock and rollers, Pete had different ideas, largely centered on his musical tastes. He had a couple of eight-track tapes he played continuously. For starters, there was the soul-sucking *Greatest Hits of Barry Manilow.* We suffered through countless choruses of, *"If you want to believe, it can be daybreak!"* and *"Oh, Mandy."* Now, I don't mean to discount the bottomless talent of Barry, but you need to understand he was *not* the rock star image I wanted to project as part of the teen male demographic of 1978. He was a much bigger hit among the female, twenty-something crowd, or even people my mom's age. But for guys like Pat and I, we were more of the Springsteen and Thorogood crowd. We liked bad boys. Barry was not a bad boy. Quite the opposite.

These musical differences were nothing we held against Pete. We recognized people were different and not everyone shared our love for loud and raucous. Pete was probably more influenced by movie soundtracks, theater show tunes and his parents' LP collection than his older siblings' Led Zeppelin and Rolling Stones LPs, like Pat and I. To make matters worse, Pete's alternative to the Manilow tape was a Dolly Parton 8-Track. Much like Barry, Dolly shattered that teen male demographic thing for me and my image. It's not that Dolly isn't an amazing talent. It's just, if Pat and I were looking for makeup, wigs and bell-bottoms, we'd be more inclined to listen to KISS than Dolly Parton.

There was something freeing about that car, though. It rolled along over the bumps and potholes of our teen life with ease. Pat always called it the "sway mobile" because of its tendency to make passengers feel like they were floating on a cloud. The ride was attributable to a combination of its suspension system and the sheer mass of the vehicle. Just sitting in it made me feel rich. Cadillacs were for the rich and for pimps. They were the pinnacle of automotive comfort and excess. So, on those occasions I had the privilege of riding in it, I appreciated everything about it. And when the top was down and the wind was in our hair and Manilow was singing "Looks Like We Made It"…well, life was *almost* perfect.

***

In part because of his father's successful career as an attorney, Pete's family lived on Summit Avenue, arguably the most prestigious street in the whole city. The avenue was lined on both sides with stately mansions and upper-class homes. The terraces in front of these homes were rich with tall, lush elms (until Dutch Elm disease did them in) that provided a beautiful soft canopy to the street. It was common knowledge if you knew someone that lived on Summit, they were doing okay, financially.

In the spring of 1979, Pete's dad, his wife and a few of their attorney friends took a vacation out of the country. His friends all left their cars parked in the long driveway in front of the carriage house at Pete's parents' residence. It was an eclectic mix of posh vehicles including a new Lincoln Continental Mark IV and a beautiful mid-'70s white Corvette. The owners left their keys at the house in case Pete needed to move them to get his dad's Cadillac out for school.

Now, I am not saying an adolescent boy shouldn't be trusted with such a great responsibility. But neither am I saying that tempting the boy with the keys to such an array of nice rides should *ever* be considered a good idea.

Unable to resist the allure of test driving a real, live Corvette, Pete showed up in front of my house one evening. He and our friend Pat came up to my door and said, "Wanna take a ride in my 'vette?"

"What? No way that is your car," was all I could muster up in my state of disbelief.

"Sure it is. Well, it's more like a loaner. So, you coming, or not?"

"Uh, yeah! Give me a second." I quickly put on my shoes and headed out the door.

"I forgot to tell you, it's a two-seater, so someone has to sit on the hump," Pete said.

"Sorry, man, last one in gets that spot," Pat informed me.

"No problem. I can squeeze in. I'll make it work."

Both Pat and I were over six feet by now, so we pretzeled ourselves into the red leather confines of the muscle car. So as to not impair Pete's ability to drive, I perched myself on the console of the interior, spilling over into Pat's lap a bit. One thing was sure. If we were looking to impress women with how cool we were in our super-horse powered white rocket, we weren't going to do it this way. It looked like a rugby scrum in the cockpit. We were a slightly cooler version of clowns crammed into a VW bug, and nothing more.

Once we were uncomfortably situated in what, for all intents and purposes, was a stolen car, Pete started the engine and we were off on our joy ride. There is no other term for it. We were joyously riding in a Corvette that wasn't ours. There's a certain lawless euphoria to something like that when you're seventeen. This was living!

Pete decided a couple of girls we knew in Eagan needed to see the car, so it became our destination. Perhaps they could see past the uncoolness of three guys in a two-seater enough to be impressed. Because, at seventeen, it's all about impressing the opposite sex.

After we worked our way down Lexington Parkway, Pete punched the accelerator a couple of times just to show us the power at his beck and call. While I was impressed by the display of pickup and performance, I thought the car handled a little rough around the city. It was a little rattly and I felt every bump and pothole on the road. I'm sure it had nothing to do with the fact that we were testing it with a weight distribution the engineers never intended due in most part to my perch on the center console. It's just a guess they never test drove the car with a third person riding shotgun to the shotgun. Automotive testers are shortsighted that way.

Bad handling aside, eventually we turned on to I-35W to cross over the Mississippi River. Because the speed limit increased to fifty five miles per hour, Pete couldn't help but unleash the beast a bit and see what she could do. He stepped hard on the gas pedal and we were all pressed back into our seats – or, in my case, into the console hump. We watched the needle rise up past seventy, eighty and ninety.

"We gotta get her up to a hundred!' I said. Our collective testosterone was building as the white ghost sped over the river below us. For as badly as the car handled at thirty-five, it recovered from its poor performance at low speed by riding like a dream in the menacing uncertainty of forty-five over the limit. It became clear this car wasn't made to putt around the city. It was made to fly! Pete continued to accelerate as we watched the needle hit 95. The last few miles per hour slid by effortlessly. The car was like a track horse that had been trotted all week and was finally free to stretch things on race day. Its thirsty engine functioned finest near the high end, pushing the tachometer to new places.

"Oh yeah! One hundred, boys!" Pete said with pride. It was probably not the first time the river had been crossed at that speed, but it certainly set a new personal record for each of us teens. It was a rush, and simultaneously, a shining example of the not-fully developed adolescent frontal cortex. I am not sure of the penalty for doing forty-five over the limit in an allegedly stolen car, but it certainly would require some of the legal counsel Pete's dad practiced for a living. However, these are the experiences that make life worth living. Was it risky? Yes. Was it stupid? Yes! But it was also a box we could check on our short list of life experiences.

Ever done a hundred in a stolen Corvette?

Why, as a matter of fact, yes I have!

***

The speed and allure of the Corvette were too much for Pete. He had to show it off a little. In part because of his house on Summit Avenue and his dad's job as a successful attorney, Pete was always a little bit of a high roller when it came to appearances and image. He liked to wear an expensive, glitzy wristwatch and carried his money in a money clip rather than a wallet. These were small things, but as a teenager they were noticeable. So, the Corvette and its extravagance fit Pete's image well.

One morning he took it to school. The Cretin boys needed to see that his array of vehicles extended beyond the convertible Cadillac Sedan Deville. Frankly the Stingray blew the caddy out of the water when it came to the cool factor. He made a point of doing a drive-by of Derham Hall on his way to school that morning. It was purposeful because fast cars and girls are a great start to any morning, even on a school day.

Corvettes always attract attention, so when one shows up on a high school campus, people notice. Unfortunately, some of those people are the administrative staff, including Bubs Boland the Dean of Discipline for our Senior year, after Brother Kevin moved on. When I ran into Pete in the hall that day he said, "Yeah, Bubs called me into his office today. Somehow he found out I was the one with the 'vette. He asked me where I got it."

"No lie? Uh, oh. What did you tell him?"

"I told him the truth. Said it was a friend of my dad's."

"What did he say to that?"

"He basically told me to not bring it around anymore this week. It is a bit of a distraction for the other students."

"Well, he's got a point there!" I laughed.

Bubs let Pete off with a warning. The two of them were on pretty good terms anyway. He'd had Bubs as a teacher for one of his classes. As a disciplinarian, Bubs was pretty lenient and fair. This incident was no different. A good guy for sure.

After the last bell of the day, Pete walked out to the car and found not one but two notes under the windshield wiper. Both notes had phone numbers and referenced the car and how the girls who wrote them would like to ride in it sometime. Pete and the rest of us were justifiably shocked and awed. From a romance standpoint, none of us had much going for us. We were all awkward, geeky teens, so any sort of female acknowledgement shown in our direction got our immediate attention. Of course, we all knew this was girls flirting with a car more than with its owner, or its thief in this case. But as I said, when girls took notice, we took notice. Heck, if it meant getting a potential date or phone number, I would have shamelessly said, "Yeah, I'm a friend of the guy with the stolen white Corvette. Yep, I'm with him."

***

Another one of the cars in Pete's driveway was a new Lincoln Continental Mark V. The car was in mint shape and featured all the newest gadgets, including an 8-track player, an automatic trunk release and a nearly soundproof interior. Like the Corvette, it was one of the vehicles that was left to "move as necessary" when the Graysons went on vacation. Strangely enough, it became necessary to move it one night, all the way to the Minnesota Twins game at Metropolitan Stadium.

Pete picked up Pat and me at our houses and we started on our way out to Eagan, where we were going to meet our friends Billy McMonigal and Dave Mayer to caravan out to the game. When I slid into the leather seats in back, I said, "Sweet ride, Pete! Leather seats, man. Another one of your dad's friends' cars?"

"Yep. Lincoln Continental, baby!"

Billy and Dave lived in Eagan, so we headed down Lexington Parkway toward the freeway and, ultimately, over the same bridge we'd crossed at a hundred miles per hour a couple of days before. Something about pricey, borrowed vehicles seemed to draw us to that bridge. When we got to Billy's house, we got out and met him and Dave outside.

"Hey guys. We got some Miller High Life and a little Boones Farm!" Billy said smiling.

I was jittery with excitement, because nothing goes better with a semi-stolen car than illegally obtained intoxicants and a trip to the old ball game. Both of those guys had a knack for acquiring alcohol, despite being only eighteen when the legal drinking age was nineteen. I was still seventeen at the time, and looked it, so was always the beneficiary of the acquisitions and never the executor. It wasn't a bad position to hold.

Billy loaded the case of beer and wine into the trunk. Pete dropped his keys into the trunk and went into the house to use the bathroom. While he was gone someone shut the trunk. Pete came back outside and quickly did the pat-down routine of someone who has misplaced their keys.

"Shit!" he said.

"What? What's up?" Pat asked.

"The keys are in the trunk. Dangit!."

"Really? Are you kidding?" I asked.

"No. I'm dead serious."

"Shit," Billy chimed in.

"Wait, I'll pop the trunk using the button!" Pete declared.

"Hey, yeah, I forgot this car has one of those," I said.

Pete hustled to the front seat and pushed the button. Nothing. He pushed it again three more times just to be sure.

"Did you push it?" Pat asked.

"Yeah, but nothing happened. It must be the key needs to be in the ignition to give power to the button."

"Well, that sucks," Dave said.

We all sat there a little befuddled as to what to do. Calling a locksmith would not only be expensive, but would attract attention to the liquor in the trunk, to say nothing of this vehicle none of us owned. We were stonewalled.

"Hey, so all we need is to get power to the button, right?" Dave said.

"Well, yeah I guess so. How do you propose to do that?" Pete asked.

"You got a battery and a couple of wires in the house, Billy?"

"Yep. Hold on, I'll run and get them."

He raced into the house.

"You really think that'll work?" I asked.

"I don't know, but we don't have many other options, do we?"

"Good point."

Billy came out with a D cell battery and a couple of wires. "How about these?"

"Yeah, that should do it. We only need a short burst of juice, so that should suffice."

Dave reclined so he could see under the dash and get at the trunk button from behind. When he found the leads, he attached the wires to them. He held everything in place and said, "Okay Pete, push the button."

Pete reached in and pushed. We heard a click and the trunk swung open. Eureka! We'd done it!

"It worked!" Pete exclaimed in triumph.

There was much backslapping and hoots all around at our brilliant success. We dodged a bullet, for sure. Thankfully we had enough collective teenage ingenuity to get us out of the jam our haste and stupidity had gotten us into.

After a few minutes, we got into the car and headed to Met Stadium. Dave and Billy lived close together, so they chose to drive together in Dave's car. Once we got to the stadium, we parked our cars, had a couple beers and went to watch the Twins. After the game, it was only ten o'clock, so, Dave mentioned we should go to the airport and play video games and pinball in the game room. It was on the way home and we all agreed that sounded like a good plan. We arranged to meet there as soon as we navigated the game traffic.

At the airport we found the game arcade near one of the gates. The room was full of blinking, flashing electronica designed to separate teens from their quarters as quickly as possible. We fanned out, each of us seeking our five minute electronic dopamine hit of choice. We plugged our quarters until we were sufficiently gamed out, then left together as a group. As we walked toward our cars in the parking lot, we discussed meeting at a different location to drink the rest of the beer and wine. When we got to our cars, I shouted "Follow us, boys!" and held up the bottle of Boones Farm, flashing it to Dave and Billy as a reminder of the fun that lay ahead.

Pat and I cracked beers from the cooler as Pete turned on the radio and we rocked on down the service road. Less than a mile later, before we were even off the airport grounds, red and blue lights flashed behind us.

"Oh shit! It's the cops! Hide those beers!" Pete said.

Pat and I put our opened beers into the cooler in the back seat while Pete pulled the car over to the shoulder. As we rolled to a stop with the cop behind us, I saw Billy and Dave passing slowly on our left, craning their necks and laughing at our predicament. Meanwhile, we sat there trying to be cool despite the feeling of dread. Pete said "I'll do all the talking, okay?"

Pat and I said, "Sure thing."

It seemed like an eternity until the cop got out of his car and approached us. In those moments, I concluded this was it. This would land me in the jail, for sure. I thought, *Lord, if you get us out of this one, I will never drink again.* There is nothing like the red and blue lights to evoke such feelings of guilt, remorse and self-examination in a person.

The cop approached the car. "Good evening, gentlemen. Do you know why I pulled you over tonight?"

"Uh, no. I wasn't speeding, was I?" Pete asked.

"No, but you rolled that stop sign back there," he said gesturing in the direction behind the car.

"Oh, sorry, Officer. I know they call those Texas Stops," Pete said trying to be all chummy. The cop nodded and asked him for his license and registration. Pete handed him his license and said he wasn't sure about the registration because this was his dad's friend's car, like that's a perfectly normal thing to happen. The cop shined his flashlight in the back seat and saw the beer cooler resting next to Pat.

"What's in the cooler?" he asked.

Pat opened the lid and showed the contents, including the two freshly-opened beers. The cop said to Pete, "Could you step out of the car, sir?"

"Yes sir," Pete replied.

The cop opened the back door and confiscated the open beers and put them on the roof of the Lincoln. He asked how many beers we had over the course of the night. Pat and I confessed we'd had maybe half a dozen between us at the Twins game. Pete was honest and said he'd not had any. The cop listened and then directed Pete to the back seat of the cruiser and began questioning him.

Back in the car, Pat and I lamented about our developing drama. "Oh crap. We are dead, man!" Pat said.

"I know. This is not good. At least Pete wasn't drinking, so we got that going for us. And it probably doesn't hurt his dad's a lawyer," I added.

"Yeah, but we're in a car that's not ours, underage, open container. Not too much positive to build on here. We're dead," Pat replied.

I couldn't help but feel he was right. I was no attorney or cop, but this would be a tough one to slip. The deck seemed stacked against us for all of our foolish choices up to this point.

Pat and I sat and waited for what seemed like an hour, though in reality, it was probably no more than ten minutes. Eventually Pete came back to the car with the cop trailing him. The cop watched as Pete dumped the open beers onto the shoulder of the road. He relinquished the rest of the unopened beer and wine and the cop walked back to the cruiser.

Pete got back into the driver's seat and breathed a huge sigh of relief as he put the key into the ignition and turned it. We were all still a little stunned at what had transpired, so we kept our conversation to relatively hushed tones.

"So, what happened? Did you get a ticket?" I asked.

"Nope. Got off with just a warning," Pete said with a slight grin.

"What? Are you kidding? Wow, did we luck out or what, man?" Pat added.

"Yeah, I told him I went to Cretin and I answered every question with sir. Kinda sucked up to him, ya know? You can never be too polite to the cops. So, after I told him I hadn't had anything to drink and this was my dad's friend's car and that they were both attorneys, he decided to let us off with a warning. He said that usually they'd arrest me, tow the car and make you two call your parents to pick you up. Thank God he was a cool cop."

Pat and I nodded our agreement as Pete pulled into traffic. We weren't sure whether the attorney reference played a part in our release, but we were all relieved to be back on the road. The cop followed behind us for a half mile or so. I think they do that intentionally to make offenders like us squirm for a while. This one was likely just checking to see if Pete swerved or crossed any lines. Eventually, he turned at an intersection when we went straight. We all sighed another sigh of relief when he stopped tailing us.

Having had enough excitement in the borrowed Lincoln, the three of us decided to head home before some other disaster happened. First the keys in the trunk incident, now this. We figured three strikes and we'd be out. Plus, the luster and appeal of the luxury car had about worn off for the night. I was shaken up and Pete and Pat were as well. We all took it as a good lesson in respect, both for other people's property and for the law.

The week of Pete's parental vacation finished out and the Lincoln's rightful owner returned to claim it, as did the owner of the Corvette. Of course Pete never mentioned any of the stories to them or his parents. In the end, the three of us had broken a handful of laws behind the wheels of the cars and come away with nothing more than a stern warning from a cop, and a few lifetime memories. It also became apparent there is some justice behind making these cars far too expensive for teenagers to afford. We were dangerous enough driving them stolen.

***

If there was an encyclopedic entry for teenage junkers, my friend Pat's 1970 Datsun 510 was it. It was a boxy, sub-compact four door with a manual transmission and a living ecosystem of rust working its way across the entire car. The car served his family well over the years, but by the time it became Pat's, the winter road salt was having its way with the vehicle's frame and slowly dismantling it.

Perhaps the most visible manifestation of the rusting decay was the right front fender. For a period of time, it flopped and shook as the nuts and bolts holding it to the frame slowly relented, one at a time. Eventually Pat removed it entirely, exposing the front suspension and wheel to the elements. The half-naked front end drew stares and smiles from people on the road when we drove around town. On the upside, if Pat ever needed to install new shocks or springs, he was halfway there.

The undercarriage of the Datsun was perilous and arguably its weakest link. The floor on both the driver and passenger sides was rusted to the point of unsafe. To step directly on the floorboards might put your foot through to the pavement. This meant getting into and out of the car required stepping on the lower door frame and the transmission hump and, preferably, nowhere in-between. Because the engine was so dependable Pat wanted to get some more miles out of the car, so he and his brothers repaired the floor using some sheet metal. Large sheets were riveted to any good steel that could be found on the frame. When it was done, it didn't make the floor much more stable, but at least passengers didn't have to watch the road speeding by underneath their feet. Pat and I used to laugh about how that feature was never a big hit on dates.

Pat's personality was always to take things outside the lines a bit, and the Datsun provided him the perfect expression of those tendencies. Both of us were big fans of *Monty Python's Flying Circus*, a popular British television series. Pat thought it would be funny if he took the opening line from the series and added it to the car. So, using a roll of masking tape he spelled out on the rear bumper the opening line from the series, "And now for something completely different…"

It was the perfect statement for the vehicle. With all of its rust, the missing fender, boxy shape and the faded red paint, it really was something completely different. Put a couple of teenagers over 6'4" in the front seat and you basically had a freak show on wheels. On one occasion, we were out driving and a car with a couple of good looking girls about our age pulled up next to us. The driver rolled down her window and said, "Hey, what does that mean on the back?"

Trying to be as cool and suave as he could, Pat shouted across to her, "It's the Monty Python thing."

The girls gave us a quizzical look like, "Wha...?" They sort of giggled, shrugged and pulled away. It seemed it was too much of an inside joke for them to understand. Pat pulled forward, turned to me and said, "Oh, well. Easy come, easy go." We both busted out laughing. After we talked about it, we agreed our wit was so sharp, our senses of humor so keen, that no one as beautiful as them could ever understand the verse and its correlation to the decrepit car. Yes, those beauties were not smart enough for the two dashing young males with their feet perched on the transmission hump of their foreign sports car. No bother. There were plenty of fish in the sea.

In his never ending quest to get another laugh, Pat took the automotive personalization routine to the next level. In a moment of artistic inspiration, he rescued a wingback chair that was destined for the trash heap, and tied it to the roof of the Datsun. He secured it facing forward as a sort of mobile throne fit for an adventurous king. I am sure there were people that thought he was just in the process of moving it for lack of a trailer, but it was much more than that. Pat was doing it simply as an extension of his uniqueness. He was not one to follow the crowd. The chair was his bowtie in a sea of neckties. His chance to stand out – or sit down, perhaps- while on the road.

I remember driving around town in his car with the chair on top and wondering what people thought. We got a kick out of watching the reactions of other drivers and pedestrians as we traversed the streets of Saint Paul. Who couldn't help but smile at a car that's missing a fender and has a little bit of the living room strapped on the roof? It was something completely different.

One of our favorite hangouts as teenagers was a place called Lee's Billiards, an alcohol free pool hall in nearby Falcon Heights. The owner, Lee, was a grizzled, lanky chain-smoker who ran a tight business overseeing a dozen pool tables for rent by the hour. "Use the coasters!" he'd shout from behind the counter after we'd purchased a can of pop from the machine. In the corner sat a jukebox thumping out the hits of the day like "My Sharona" and "Sultans of Swing," while teens and twenty-somethings circled the tables calculating angles and putting their high school geometry skills to the test. The smoky, sometimes rollicking confines were a portal to adulthood and we spent lots of time and money there pushing ourselves to the other side.

One summer evening as Pat and I were engaged in another gripping match of last pocket, a patron came in and asked who owned the car with the chair on top and the Monty Python quote on the bumper?

Pat looked at me, cracked up and said, "That would be me."

"Well, you left your lights on."

His identification of the car was certainly more definitive than asking who owns a rusty red compact.

The rooftop chair was a novel idea for a week, but after the initial zaniness wore off, Pat decided to test out the engineering stability of the elevated rumble seat. He somehow convinced his younger brother Matt to take a seat on the throne-of-death atop the decrepit import for a test run around the neighborhood. Matt climbed up in the armchair and held on tight as Pat slowly cruised the streets. It was automotive version of a wing-walker aerial act. The roof sitter! When I asked Matt what it was like, he said it was both exhilarating and wildly terrifying. As it turned out, somewhere along the line one of the neighbors recognized the car as it passed and later informed Pat and Matt's parents. Pat's father made him take the chair off and gave him a lecture on the responsibilities that come with owning your own car. Wingback chair roof-surfing wasn't part of taking those responsibilities seriously. Who knew?

Eventually, Pat's dad found a case of empty beer bottles in the trunk. Because we were still underage, he took Pat's car ownership privileges away for good. The car was eventually sold for scrap and, in all of its rusted glory, squashed up and returned to the earth. Pat went on to own a number of sketchy vehicles over the next ten years of his life, including a couple of Volkswagen Beetles I played a role in helping him render useless. One died a fiery death to an engine fire on our way to Saint Cloud. The other was irreversibly hobbled when we jumped a construction barrier on a rainy night while we were both wearing sunglasses. We were nothing in our youth if not automotively reckless. Stories for another time, I suspect.

But of all Pat's cars, I'll always remember that Datsun the most. With its multitude of inglorious quirks, it was the embodiment of my best friend's personality. Like him, it was outside the mainstream and had character, flair and a sense of humor about it. It went the extra mile through the hard times with us and, despite its bad complexion, was loveable. To some people, a car is a tool, a way to get from point A to point B. But to us, the Datsun was more like an old friend.

CHAPTER 17: JOBS

Four out of six of the kids in my family attended private schools. My older brother, Tom and I went to Cretin and my sisters, Pat and Jane went to Saint Agnes and Brady. This choice was one mom made, and we are all grateful she did, but it did pose a financial hardship for her. Tuition at Cretin was certainly more affordable than Saint Thomas, our competitor across the Mississippi River, but still presented a challenge to an already tight household budget. Mom's answer to this was to encourage each of us to work a part time job at some point during our high school years to help pay tuition. I vividly remember her telling me, "Tom paid his whole tuition junior and senior years, you can certainly do your share."

My first job opportunity came during my freshman year, when my brother Tom mentioned that TuWay, a combination gas station/car wash where he worked, was hiring. He promised me it was simple work, pumping gas and operating the automatic car wash. They were paying two dollars and twenty five cents an hour and I could work there a couple of nights a week from four until eight o'clock, when they closed. His buddy's parents owned the place and a classmate of mine, Chris Wildasin, also worked there, so it seemed like a perfect fit.

At the time, I was only fourteen years old and not exactly oozing with confidence. I spent my first few evenings shadowing my classmate, Chris, as he showed me the ropes. He and I sat in the office and waited until cars pulled up to the pumps. We'd run out, ask whether they wanted regular or premium and how much, then pump the gas for them. This part of the job was brain dead easy, but as a kid who was nervous about working his first job and doing things right, I managed to mess up a few times.

Once a guy pulled up in a mint-condition Corvette and asked me to fill it up with premium. High performance cars back then ran much better with high octane gas and the Corvette was certainly the pinnacle of high performance. Coming from a family of Chevys and Chryslers,

I knew nothing of such highbrow needs. Because ninety percent of my customers took regular, I started the pump. I was half done filling it before the guy noticed and said, "Hey, you are filling it with *premium*, right?"

"Ooops! No. Sorry, that was regular," I said grabbing the pump and stopping it.

"Oh, my god, really? You do realize this car needs premium, right? Oh, my god, kid. Could you do me a favor and fill the rest with premium? I'll have to hope for the best from there. Geez." He was seething.

It was my first disgruntled customer. I am pretty sure this is why they encourage kids to wait until at least sixteen to start working in the service industry.

On a different occasion, a regular stopped in for his once a week fill-up. He was a jovial, middle-aged guy who always greeted me with, "Hiya, Tiger. Fill it up." It was refreshing to have someone so positive come to the station on a weekly basis. I think he liked the fact I was so green behind the ears, just a kid really, so he always made an attempt to be upbeat. Because he was so nice, I tried to make small talk with him as the gas was pumping. One evening after I'd filled his tank I thought I'd let him in on what my boss had told me in the office an hour before.

"Hey, the good news is tomorrow our gas is going down by ten cents a gallon!"

"What? Are you kidding me? Why didn't you tell me that before you started pumping this tank?" he asked with a definite edge to his tone.

"Um, I uh. Ooops. Sorry about that," I said, recognizing my gaff.

But the gentleman I only knew as "Tiger Guy" would have none of it. He paid me and drove away in a huff. It was a good business lesson for me as a young employee in the working world. I learned that next time I would keep my good news to myself, keep the small talk to weather and sports. Perhaps even more importantly, I also learned some people were only as nice as the next bad transaction.

***

The car wash machine at TuWay had a mind of its own. It was an automated unit that wheeled itself back and forth after the car was

129

driven into the bay and the garage doors were shut. There were five brushes, two on each side, one covering the lower part of the car, the other the windows, and one for the roof. During my training on how to operate it, I was told when the brushes got near the hood of the car you had to push down on one relief valve and pull up on another. Doing this stopped the upper brush from spinning and was used to prevent car antennas and side view mirrors from being pummeled and bent at non-factory angles.

One evening, I had a gentleman pull into the car wash bay with a souped-up Dodge Challenger. The vehicle was in mint condition, but in need of a wash. I directed the guy in and told him to shut off the engine. I flicked the switch and the machine made its first pass, just a rinse. On the second pass, the huge brushes began to spin and whir. They whipped the body of the Dodge and began to strip away the layer of crud that comes courtesy of a Minnesota winter. As they moved past the passenger window, I pulled and pushed the relief valves, as I was shown, to stop the upper brushes from spinning. To my surprise, they kept whirring right on past me as I gazed through the window.

Now, I had done this same exercise a handful of times before without incident. So I was understandably dumbfounded when the machine didn't function as it did in the past. I watched helplessly as the car wash whipped the radio antenna into submission. In my panic, I pushed and pulled the valve stopper again in hopes the upper brushes would stop, to no avail. I breathed a sigh of relief as the antenna whipped back and forth but emerged unscathed after the brushes passed. It looked like I dodged a bullet this time, like the worst was behind me.

As it continued on, the brushes scrubbed the front fender of the muscle car squeaky clean. Knowing it would be a few more minutes, I went back to sitting in the office while the automatic washer finished. When it was done, I pushed the button and the overhead door buzzed and clacked open and the car pulled out, but didn't drive off.

The driver got out and walked around to the office door and came in.

"Did you see what your car wash did to my car?"

"Uh, no. What happened?" I asked.

"Come on out and I'll show you," the customer said irately.

We walked out to his car and he took me to look at his hood ornament. The custom-made flying bird hood ornament sat there cockeyed, forty-five degrees off center. It begged to be grabbed and twisted back into place. The owner stood there distraught and fuming. He approached the car and attempted to correct the issue. He managed to get the ornament nearly into alignment, but it just didn't look quite like it did before. It sat just a little bit off-kilter. I felt horrible, but unfortunately the damage was done.

"Uh, I'm really sorry about this, sir," I said.

"Awww, cripes! Yeah, whatever, guy," he said, waving me off as he continued to try to wrestle the hood ornament into its original configuration. It was clear my groveling was not going to help soothe his aggravation, so I slinked back to the confines of the office. Later that week, the owners of TuWay told me they heard from the customer and they offered to help pay the thirty dollars to fix the ornament. They reminded me how the wash worked and seemed less than convinced it was a mechanical failure. In the end, I think it was a bit of a wake-up call on the hazards of hiring fourteen-year old attendants.

To be honest, I never liked the responsibility of running the entire operation on my own. At night, I was in charge of closing the place, counting the money, checking total fuel sales, locking pumps and doors, cleaning the car wash bays, and on and on. It just seemed like a lot at my young age. None of this was to preclude the ever present threat of a hold-up, which was always there in the back of my mind, as well.

So, when high school track season came in the spring, I used it as my excuse to quit the job at TuWay. I probably could have managed my time between practices, meets and work, but I was looking for an out. My days at TuWay were a learning experience for sure, and I mean more than just the difference between regular and premium. I learned that for a variety of reasons, I was ill-suited for a life in the service industry. Working with the public just wasn't for me. Most of all though, it was a job that was a stark reminder of the importance of getting a good education so I could rise above pumping gas and reorienting hood ornaments.

***

As I mentioned previously, another part time job I held in high school was working at the Lexington, a black tie restaurant a few blocks from my house. The manager of the place, Don Ryan, lived across the street from us and his son Pat was a friend of mine, so I had an automatic in. (It also seems I had an affinity for friends with the name Pat.) A couple of buddies both worked there and were always commenting on how good the money was. After a little of their encouragement, I applied and was hired as a dishwasher. During my Junior and Senior years I held a variety of positions there.

Dishwasher was the lowest of the low kitchen positions. It was hot, dirty work and on weekend nights, it got extremely busy as trays full of dirty dishes from the dining room started backing up on the sorting counter. The station was a two man operation, one at the counter emptying trays and another in "the hole," scraping garbage into the disposal and stacking everything methodically before a run through the industrial dishwasher. The two person team was assisted during these "run times" by a third person, usually the pot washer. He typically took over the tray clearing while that guy moved to the "catching off" spot where the clean dishes came out and were stacked. It was a noisy but well-orchestrated and efficient process.

Dishwashers were also tasked with keeping the chefs stocked with plates behind their service counters. Our white uniform coats bonded us "pearl divers" with the chef's as the hardworking brotherhood of the kitchen. The chefs at the Lexington were a bunch of good guys. While we toiled behind the noise and steam of the dishwasher, they had the hot, stressful work of taking orders from the demanding waitstaff. The kitchen's night crew was led by John Donnelly, a heavy-set head chef. John was one of the most upbeat people I ever worked with. He kept things light by joking with the waitstaff and us lowly dish folk.

One particular night I got a taste of John's sense of humor, firsthand. At the start of our shift, the initial setup involved prepping the dishwashing station for the evening. As part of this, we drained the silverware rinsing sink and refilled it with fresh water. The water was heated with a gas burner to scalding-hot temperatures to ensure the cutlery was sterilized and well-rinsed after it was run through the washer. After draining the water and carrying out some other tasks, I ordered a burger and went on my pre-shift dinner downstairs in the break room. Halfway through my burger, my dishwashing co-worker Pete and I got an urgent call from John over the intercom system, "Hey, dishwashers, come on up here. We've got a fire!"

Pete and I dropped what we were eating and dashed toward the stairs. We sprinted up the steps two at a time and turned the corner into the kitchen area. "What's going on? Where's the fire?" I asked. John stood there calmly with a huge grin on his face. He laughed and said, "Oh, there's no fire. But there could have been. One of you left the burner on underneath the silverware sink after you drained out the water. The sumbitch was smoking hot!" I walked over to the sink and could feel the residual heat coming off the bottom.

"I turned it off, of course, but thought I'd give you a good scare so you don't make that mistake again," John said.

I stood there with Pete, stunned. We'd been punked for sure, but it was for a good cause, so it was hard to be upset. The other cooks had a good laugh at our oversight. Being the new kids on staff, we were fair game for things like this. It kept life in the busy kitchen light and fun. Being a chef or fry cook in a successful black-tie restaurant had moments of great stress. Blowing off a little steam at the expense of the high schoolers was their way of venting the kettle.

***

The Lexington had little micro communities within it. At a high level, there was the dining room staff and there was the kitchen help. One dealt with the public and had to be on their best game, the other was to be invisible to customers. While both groups were stressed during the busy times, neither one had much sympathy for the other. There was an underlying mutual respect, but when the performance of one is gauged on the performance of the other, well, things got testy at times. Furthermore, if you started your job in the kitchen and then moved to working the dining room, you were considered a turncoat and were now playing for the enemy.

As staff turned over or moved on to other positions, dishwashers were encouraged to move up to either a different post in the kitchen or on to the waitstaff. Pat and Pete both took different directions when the opportunity arose. As my chance to advance came up, they both encouraged me to join their side. Pat chose the kitchen route, moving from dishes to a spot as a salad chef. The restaurant did so much business on weekends there were usually two people working this station, and even then, they were kept busy practically the whole night.

The crew was responsible for multiple kinds of salads as well as club sandwiches, BLTs and desserts.

Pete, on the other hand, went from dishwasher to busboy. This was an arguably more refined position requiring a pressed white shirt, black dress pants, vest and bowtie. Busboys were tasked with the clearing and setting of tables, stocking the bar with glasses and ice and helping the waitstaff serve meals. The serving involved hauling large, heavy trays of hot food hoisted above their shoulder with one hand. When dinner was done, the busboys cleared the dishes and set trays of them on the counter in front of the dishwashers for scraping and washing. In essence, much of the service flow at the Lex, as we called it for short, was heaped upon the shoulders of low-wage, high school teenagers.

Initially, I sided with Pat and his push to work alongside him at the salad station. I moved into the position and under his tutelage learned the difference between Romaine and Iceberg lettuce, between too much dressing, versus just the right amount, and the litany of ingredients that go into a Cobb. I also learned about deveining shrimp for shrimp cocktail, peeling it for shrimp scampi, and how to remove the skin from Sole, a fish I'd never heard of before. I dreaded nights where sole skinning was necessary, as the abrasive skin of the fish gave the underside of my forearms a red rash. Sole skinning was soul skinning, so to speak.

On nights Pat was off, I worked alongside a guy named Tim Knipe who lived in my neighborhood. He was a year older than me and was a hard worker. I looked up to him because he seemed like a tough guy who also had an air of coolness about him. Problem was, his great work ethic came along with the baggage of a hot temper. He was a moody one. I was always careful to test his mood early on in the night. If he came in with a good disposition, I was in for an easy, productive and potentially fun night. But if he came in dragging his black cloud in tow, look out.

During high volume times on a Friday night, when he was pressured by the waiters and waitresses, he sometimes blew his stack. His favorite target for his outrage was the industrial-sized toaster. He took to punching the side of it in moments of anger. This was usually accompanied by a good four-letter curse. Ultimately, the outbursts hurt Tim more than the appliance, but I think that was the point. It showed a level of toughness, a degree of moxie to himself, if no one else. When people witnessed Tim's outbursts, they treaded lightly around the salad station until the emotional storm lifted.

He was also a fairly reckless guy. One night he just didn't show up for work. Pat later found out it was because he jumped a train and ended up somewhere outside of town. That pretty much summed up the angst and randomness of Tim. Too much teen energy for his own good.

***

I didn't stay much longer than a few months at the salad station. The life of a busboy seemed far more appealing and glamorous than that of a lowly salad chef. The promise of nightly tips, a cash kickback from each of the waitstaff and a cleaner, higher profile job seemed alluring to me. Of course, that thinking was delusional, work is work and all restaurant jobs are pretty stressful, so you just sort of change positions up the ladder moving from one set of stresses to another.

Weekends at the Lex usually meant one or more large parties in the Williamsburg dining room. They were wedding rehearsal dinners, anniversary celebrations, birthdays for the rich, etc. They usually designated one busboy specifically to work these events. Things ran fairly methodically for parties. The busboys started by bringing large trays of waters and setting one for each patron. Then, the same routine was done for soup, salad, dinner and dessert. It was feeding in large volume and meant a lot of coordination between kitchen help and the party staff to ensure the salads were served cool, the food hot, and everyone was kept fed and watered.

There were automatic doors that functioned between the kitchen and the dining room. It was triggered by a sweet spot in the floor that, when stepped on, swung the doors outward toward the dining room for a couple of seconds while the person passed through. The unknown variable was, this switch was a little dodgy at times. If you had momentum and happened to miss the sweet spot, the doors would stay closed requiring you slow your progress and feel around with your foot until you hit the spot. Another scenario was, if you didn't step on the spot quite long enough, the doors would open and then shut in half the normal time. It was a timing thing that took some getting used to.

On a busy Friday night, I was assigned as the party room busboy. Dishes clanked and clattered, waiters and waitresses shouted orders at the chefs and great clouds of steam and smoke billowed from the deep fryers and grills, only to be sucked skyward by the hoods overhead. Across from the dishwashers, Terry, the service bartender, poured drink orders for staff to rush to tables in the dining room. Weekend evenings were always frenetic affairs of organized chaos at the Lex, and this one was no different.

After delivering salads, I was tasked with helping to deliver the French onion soup to the party. My attendant waiter and I filled our big steel serving trays with twelve cups of soup with matching saucer under liners and rushed them out to the party. After my first trip, the party waiter reminded me there were four more soups that needed to come in from the kitchen. I acknowledged his request and returned to get them. I grabbed a much smaller plastic service tray and put the four cups waiting under the kitchen warmer onto it. Because these trays were much smaller, the preferred method of carrying them was underhanded out in front of your body.

As I hurried into the hallway leading to the dining room, I stepped on the door opener not realizing I hadn't held my step long enough. The doors jerked open as I headed through them leading with my tray. Before I had the chance to follow, the doors slapped shut on my arm. I was helpless as the tray tipped and I could feel the cups of soup slide off. As everything dropped to the floor, I struggled to wrest my arm from the doors squeezing it. I heard the dishes clang to the ground as I envisioned my impending pink slip and kicked around ideas about my new career options. It was one thing to drop a tray of dirty dishes, but to drop one with food on it meant you weren't only breaking dishes, but wasting food, as well.

I managed to slide my foot around and find the door opener spot to free myself. A couple of waitresses came rushing to my aid and helped me sort out the broken cups from the unbroken. One of them brandished a couple of service towels and soaked up the soup from the carpet.

"I'm so sorry. These danged doors closed without my being able to control them," I pleaded to anyone who would listen.

"Oh, I know honey. I hate those things sometimes. They're so sensitive."

Between us, we cleaned up the mess under the watching eyes of nearly everyone in the dining room. It's pretty amazing the attention a dropped tray of dishes will attract, most of it in sympathy from the gawkers. No one likes to see anyone put in that kind of position.

After we cleaned up the mess, I was approached by Mr. Ryan, the restaurant manager. He wanted to make sure I was okay and to remind me that next time I should make sure the doors were fully engaged before walking through them. It was a reminder I didn't really need, but, hey, thanks. And, while this was perhaps the lowest point in my relatively short run at the Lex, I couldn't help but wonder what it must have looked like from the dining room. A random arm holding a tray full of soups extending out from the kitchen, only to have a door close. It was like something straight out of the Adams Family. Frankly, by the end of my two years at the Lexington, I was certain I did not want a job in the food business. It was not my thing.

CHAPTER 18: GIRLS!

There were a few things Cretin was not. The most obvious, of course, was it was not a great source of male/female socialization. Granted, there was an all-girl's school, Derham Hall, just a grassy football field length away. But that distance may as well have been a crocodile-filled moat called No Man's Land. Those of us who were shy were certainly not going to cross the great divide between testosterone and estrogen to prowl around the grounds of Derham on our lunch hour, looking for a date. The administrators tended to frown on that, particularly the nuns.

When people hear I attended an all-male, military, Catholic school, they are usually a little shocked. After we talk about the specifics, however, the question usually comes up; would I attend the same school if I had the chance to do it over again? My answer is always a definitive no. It has nothing to do with the educational quality, or the religious and military requirements. I'll be blunt. It's all about girls! And not in the sense you might think. Rather, I am a firm believer in the fact that being around girls helps boys mature faster. It's a well-known fact girls mature earlier than boys. So, when there are no girls present, I think the emotional maturity of adolescent males gets stunted. With girls around, we're kept in check. We simply do not want to look immature in front of them.

Both Cretin and Derham Hall did make attempts to mix the sexes of the two schools on occasion. One type of event was the inter-school dances held a few times a year. They were called "mixers" and typically involved charging students a few dollars to get in to dance to a DJ or a live band in the school gymnasium. While it was amazing being among a bunch of good looking girls my age, from my perspective, mixers were mostly a gathering of them in their cliques on one side of the gym and us hanging out in our clumps on the other.

I remember the highlight of one dance was a crowd of people circled around Jim Morelli who was doing an amazing solo dance to the song "Car Wash." His moves were phenomenal. He started with the Robot, jerking mechanically looking exactly like something out of Lost in Space. Then, at one point he dropped to his knees, fell backward and pulled himself back upright hand over hand using an imaginary rope. My friends and I stood there in awe clapping to the beat and cheering him on. It was an incredible performance, but also a sort of metaphor for the evening. Here we were, supposed to be mixing and dancing with the opposite sex, and what were we doing? Hanging out with our buddies watching one guy dance alone. With no disrespect to Jim's talent, from a socialization perspective, it was actually pretty pathetic.

***

To its credit, Cretin did do a decent job when it came to high school formal dances. In January of my senior year, they coordinated with Regina, a Catholic all-girl school in Minneapolis, to match up boys with girls for Regina's Sno Ball dance. This was in the era before internet dating sites and social media, so we were paired by height. In retrospect, I understand what they were trying to do. The last thing you want at a blind date dance is to have a girl that is 6'3" paired up with a guy that is 5'4". So, I guess it was a legitimate criteria.

My last two years in high school I hit a growth spurt and shot up to 6'4". I noted it and a few other details on the dance form and hoped for the best. I wondered if there were ever any studies done to determine if height was a unifying quality – a commonality that bridged some sort of relational chasm and brought two people together based on nothing more than the length of their inseam. Probably not, and it didn't really matter anyway. I was looking for a date to a dance, not a life partner.

A few days after submitting our names, addresses and heights, those of us in this lottery of love were notified of our matchups. I ended up with a tall brunette, Marcia Laam. We were given the girls' phone numbers and left to make the initial connection and subsequent dance arrangements between us.

I hemmed and hawed for days before making the first phone call. Sadly, I hadn't really had a girlfriend by this point in my life, due in part to my seclusion among my Catholic military brethren, so any sort of contact, even over the phone, was fairly daunting. None of it was made

139

easier by the fact that I'd never even seen her. I wondered what she'd look like, as any superficial seventeen-year-old would. Would she be fat or thin? Geeky or smart? Would she walk with a limp, stutter or chew with her mouth open? Then again, she could be stunning and beautiful, out of my league. This option might be the worst-case scenario. The last thing I needed was to be dismissed as not good or cool enough. I just didn't know what to expect from this mystery girl.

Before the call, I rehearsed over and over in my head what I would say and talk about. Her family, her college aspirations, musical tastes, sports, etc. I feared and worried about the dreaded awkward pauses, an occurrence that was almost certain to happen when two strangers converse for the first time. Thinking about all the dreadful conversational trip-ups was almost worse than actually carrying out the action. Eventually I secluded myself in a bedroom and called her. We talked for fifteen minutes or so, and from what I could tell of her voice, she seemed nice enough. We made a date to go out for pie and coffee at Baker's Square near her house in Minneapolis. The thought was, it would give us a good chance to get to know one another a little better before the dance. The pie place seemed non-threatening enough, so it was set.

I pulled into the parking lot of Baker's Square and got out of the Volare'. As vehicles go, it was an embarrassing mode of transportation. In the first few years after purchasing it, the car had a number of factory recalls, not the least of which was a complete replacement of both front fenders which rusted badly just two years after the car was purchased. The cars were exemplary of everything Chrysler did badly in the late '70s, and certainly one of the biggest automotive industry lemons of all time. It was a girl magnet with reversed polarity. If I was going to woo Marcia based solely on the car I drove, this would surely be a one date relationship.

I walked in and looked around. Based on the description she'd given me, I didn't see her. The hostess came and led me to a booth near a window so I could watch for her. Within five minutes, a girl walked up to my booth and said, "And, you must be Jim."

"Yes, I am. And you must be Marcia?"

"Yep."

I rose from my seat and gave her a hug.

True to the match criteria, she stood tall at about 5' 10", her brunette hair in a cute Dorothy Hamill-length bob cut. As appearances went, it seemed evident I'd met my perfect match. She was attractive in a girl-next-door sort of way as much as I was handsome in a my-brother-is-more-handsome-but-I-ain't-bad sort of way. Not stunning, but good looking. She slid into the booth seat facing me. After the initial awkwardness, we hit a groove and ended up finding a comfort level with one another.

We ordered pie and pop and proceeded to talk for an hour and a half. It was strangely pleasant. I was still a kid, seventeen at the time, (youngest in my grade) but yet I was doing a very adult thing. It was one-to-one and, for all intents and purposes, my first date. I asked about her family, her studies and hobbies. She returned the courtesy and asked about mine. We laughed, ate our desserts and slurped pop through straws. My head was filled with curiosity about what she thought of me. Was I coming across as trying too hard? Was I not talking enough? Was there pie crust in my teeth? One thing was sure, this was harder than hanging out with my buddies. I never needed to impress them.

When we were done, I asked for the check and said I would pay it. She objected momentarily, then thanked me when I insisted. I hugged her goodbye and said, "Well, this was fun. It was really nice to get to know you a little before the dance."

"Yes, it was. I had fun," she said.

As I drove home I replayed the night over in my head. I'd never had the attention of a girl for that long before and it felt really good. It was just nice being alone with one. Cretin and its male-only environment had grown wearisome and this was a nice change. When it came right down to it, we were just a couple of nervous teens working out those first date jitters. We were learning the give and take of interaction, and in the process watching to see if there was any spark at all. From my seat, I thought it was a relative success. I could only hope Marcia thought the same.

***

On the night of the Sno Ball dance, I was a bundle of nerves. I dressed in my brand new rust-colored corduroy three piece suit with the bell-bottom pants and a pair of uncomfortable, square-toed dress shoes. I'd picked out my fashion finery at Rosedale mall and paid a whopping $89.00 for it, not including tailoring costs. It was a lot of money at the time, especially for a kid bussing tables at the Lexington for $2.50 an hour plus tips. Having never been to a formal dance, I knew this was my big chance to impress, so I spared no expense. Rust colored corduroy it was!

I picked up Marcia about a half hour before our dinner reservations. When I met her at the door, she was dressed in a conservative skirt and blouse befitting a nice Catholic girl. Practical, functional and, on this night, beautiful in a matter-of-fact way. We drove to the Steak and Ale restaurant and met up with a few of her girlfriends and their dates. It was an equally odd and liberating experience, feeling all grown up and adult-like, yet gawky and nervous. We were a scene from every high school dance ever, all of us boys in our suits escorting our lottery-determined rent-a-dates in their dresses, skirts and corsages. We ate fancy food like steak tenderloins and iceberg lettuce salads with French dressing. When the bill for the two of us came, I grabbed it and, once again insisted on paying. This was my gig and another chance at nobility.

When we arrived at Regina, we checked in at the door and were shuffled over to the photo area. We stood awkwardly, arms around each other's waists, trying to look comfortable. I was unsure how tightly to grip her, how close to lean in, without being obtrusive. I wanted us to look good but was also trying to figure out if this relative stranger was someone I'd feel compelled to continue to see after this dance. It was the first time I'd even remotely embraced a girl in a relational way and it felt right and good. For the moment, maybe just the next few hours, I had myself a girl. It was my own seventeen-year-old coming out party and I was just happy to be there.

We went into the auditorium. It was decked out with streamers, soft lighting and tables with chairs on the edge of a large dance floor sprinkled with sawdust. The band on the stage played top-40 hits from the late seventies and were doing a pretty good job of it. Being a music buff, I was happiest out on the dance floor. I badgered Marcia to dance every few songs or so as the music took me away. I favored the faster dances where we danced a few feet from one another, each of us cutting our own groove. We took breaks, drank fruit punch and talked over the music when the crappy songs came on.

Late in the evening, the band struck up the first few notes of Steely Dan's, "FM," and I said, "Oh, I love this song. Wanna dance?"

"Sure!" Marcia said.

We got up and shook it together as the band worked through the jazz-rock radio hit with coolness and gym band perfection. They played it with no static at all as we bobbed and twisted, cut and dug. It was post-disco, conservative, white kids dancing to be sure, but we made it fun and kept from embarrassing ourselves. I tried to lead as much as that is even possible from three feet apart. Mostly it involved an occasional change in direction along with efforts to keep us from drifting into other couples' circles. As we danced, I was completely swept away in happiness unlike I'd ever experienced.

Now it's hard to say what made that Steely Dan dance moment so strikingly memorable for me. It might have just been the whole first dance with a girl thing. Or, maybe it was the song. Or maybe, just maybe, it was the realization that my days as a boy were behind me. That this was a little taste of what it was like to be a man. To compliment a truly good, deserving woman, and treat her with dignity and respect. To give her a flower, make her feel beautiful, open doors for her, and share a meal together. It was a coming-of-age moment of sorts, and I knew it. And, at seventeen, it was just a little bit of perfection.

Marcia and I had such a good time at Sno Ball we agreed to be partners at the Cretin Midwinter dance a month later. Despite getting along great at this dance too, somehow we drifted and eventually lost contact. Part of the problem was she was nearly a thirty minute drive away. My friend Pat used to call girls like this "GU". Geographically Undesirable. It was nothing against her personally, it's just that trying to date a girl who lives that distance away while sharing Mom's car with her and two other siblings required a bit more coordination than I had energy for. To add to the matter, she was headed to Creighton University in Nebraska the following fall, so that reality loomed as well. None of this took away the fact that we would always have those awkward but magical nights together of those formal dances in our senior year. Nights I didn't want to end.

***

On the other end of the dance experience spectrum for me was an event called Officers' Ball. This was a joint event between four schools: Cretin, Saint Thomas, Derham Hall and Visitation. Saint Thomas was our rival male, Catholic military school just across the Mississippi

River. Their accompanying girl's academy was Visitation. For this dance, any student who achieved the rank of officer was welcome to attend. I was a second lieutenant officer by then and thought it would be a good chance to meet a girl and have a fun evening. Like Sno Ball, boys who did not have a date and still wanted to go, could enter their name in a lottery and be paired up with a girl from either Derham or Visitation.

With Marcia out of the picture, I had no date for the ball. As a result, my name was again dumped into the grab bag of loneliness and romantic desperation for matching with an equally lonely and desperate girl. I was matched up with Michelle. It seems these lottery systems were stacked with girls whose names started with the letter M.

I don't remember much about the phone call exchanges between Michelle and me, which makes me think they were kept short and awkward. I do know she had a girlfriend who was going with a classmate of mine, Larry Brown, and they wanted to go to the ball together as a double date. Larry Brown was a relative stranger to me, even after four years in the same school. We both just hung in different circles and never really got to know each other. So it wasn't just a blind date, but it was a double date with a guy I didn't really hang out with. Let's stack all the bad variables up in a nice tower of disappointment, shall we? No potential problems with this scenario. Should be a blast!

It was a cold, clear winter afternoon when I picked up Larry in Mom's Volare'. He was a big, stocky dude and, although we hadn't ever spoken to each other at school, we managed to make small talk on the way to his date's house. After a few long pauses in our conversation, I got the impression he was here to date his girlfriend and didn't see this as a great chance to develop a new friendship. Knowing you will probably never speak to a guy again after the dance makes for a difficult conversation and a long evening.

We picked up Larry's date, Barb, and the three of us headed over to Michelle's house. I parked in her driveway. The snowbanks of the drive were piled high from another brutal Minnesota winter. The air had a crisp bite to it and my breath vaporized on contact. I rang the bell and waited. Michelle's mother answered, let me in and we introduced ourselves. After a bit, Michelle came into the room. She was blond, slim and attractive in her formal ball gown. Our first words felt stiff, forced and disingenuous. It was nothing like the warmth I felt with Marcia a few months prior. I have a pretty good perception for what people are thinking, and my gut feeling here was not warm and fuzzy.

I pinned her corsage to her gown and, after a picture or two, we climbed into my pimpin' Plymouth. As the driver of three strangers in my car, I was a bundle of nerves. To add to the matter, I hadn't driven much in winter. As I backed the car out of the narrow driveway, I cut the corner too tight and managed to get my right rear wheel stuck in the snowbank near the street. I gunned the engine only to spin the wheel and dig it deeper.

"Uh oh. I don't like the sound of that," I said.

"Try rocking it, Jim," Larry said from the back seat.

I worked the shifter on the steering column with fury and intent. Drive. Reverse. Drive. Reverse. My efforts only met with more spinning tires, the faint smell of burning rubber and an apparent disdain from my date. Michelle sat there looking annoyed as I tried to hero my way out of the jam I worked myself into.

After a couple of minutes of putting the Plymouth's transmission through the paces, I sat there, helpless.

"Looks like we might need a push."

Larry sighed and said, "I'll push. You try and rock it out."

From a military standpoint, he actually outranked me at the time. He was a first lieutenant and I was a second. If we were in the army, he probably could have pulled rank on me and made me push. Of course, life at Cretin was "military lite," and rank really meant nothing outside the walls of school. So, he opened the door and harrumphed his way out into the cold. Then, in his military uniform and black polished dress shoes he assumed the winter position known all too well by Minnesotans. Crouching near the trunk and holding onto the back fender, he leaned into the car and said, "Okay, remember to rock it. Hit it!"

I gunned the slant six engine forward and with Larry's heft and strength, we managed to move it a couple of inches. I let up and we rocked backwards. I repeated the gunning and releasing as we got the Volare' into that second most popular joyous rhythm that brings a smile to northerners in those parts. After about four good rocks, I was able to ease the car into the driveway. Larry came back around the passenger side, stamped the snow off his dress shoes and climbed in back next to his date.

"Nice work, thanks. Sorry about that."

"Yeah, no problem," he said curtly. He'd not only pushed us out of a snowbank, but he'd pushed aside any likelihood we'd ever develop into friends. Between him and Michelle, the mood in the car was beginning to reflect the iciness of the weather this winter evening.

The dinner and dance were both held at the Prom Center in Saint Paul. It was a romantic setting featuring a large ballroom with a stage up front and a bar and lounge in the back. The patterned carpet, ornate overhead light fixtures and heavy wallpaper gave the place a rich, albeit dated feel. It was the type of place your parents would go to listen to big band music in the fifties and sixties. Judging from the instrumental setup on stage, it appeared this evening we would be subjected to the same musical genre our parents had danced to. This was yet another letdown for me as I favored rock and considered this music highly uncool, a relic of a generation prior.

After a half hour of socializing with friends we settled in around a big table for dinner. We were seated with a mix of officers from Saint Thomas and their dates, serving to make already forced conversations even more difficult. I wondered how much small talk I could make with guys from a rival school without sounding fake or contrived. Besides, I disliked Tommies. They were Cretin's arch rivals! Furthermore, the conversation with Michelle up to this point was still stiff and obligatory. I was beginning to wish I'd skipped the privilege of being part of such a joyous celebration of the high falutin' officer brass.

When dinner was finished, the band started up and couples drifted out to the dance floor. I was really not digging the musical choice for the evening, but there was little I could do about it at this point. I turned to Michelle, "Would you like to dance?"

"Sure," she replied.

We slinked our way out to the floor and I did my best to look like I knew what I was doing. This was a new gig for me, but I discovered if you've got a decent sense of rhythm you can fake it when you need to. Michelle swayed along and appeared indifferent to the possibility of having fun with any of it. I wasn't sure if the whole stuck-in-the-driveway thing doomed me for the rest of the night, but it certainly appeared to be shaping up that way.

After a couple more lame attempts on the crowded dance floor, and one invitation where she turned me down, she asked if it was okay if she went and talked to a couple of friends a few tables away.

"Sure, no problem," I told her. It seemed she was looking for a reprieve from her commitment, and to be honest, the way things were going, so was I. She wandered away and after a few minutes of sitting there alone, I sought out my friend Pete, who was with his girlfriend, Amy.

"Hey, guys, what's up?" I said.

"Not much, Jim. Where's your date?" Pete asked.

"Oh, she's talking to some friends across the way."

"How's it going so far?"

"Well, she IS over there and I'm over here…" I reminded him sarcastically.

Pete nodded. "That good, eh? Well, have a chair."

I got a chair and talked to Pete and Amy for a half an hour or so. I kept checking back at my table to see if Michelle had returned or not. No dice.

"Well, I'd better get back. Good talking to you two."

Eventually, Michelle returned and we chatted for a while. After another obligatory dance, she asked again if it was okay to go and hang with her friends. She spent another half hour over by them while I wandered around, visited the restroom and tried to look like I was having fun. When it came time to leave, Michelle heard of an after-dance party on Summit Avenue, a street renowned for its stately mansions and high income residences. It sounded okay to me, so I obliged in hopes of salvaging something of the evening. Larry and Barb weren't interested, so I dropped them off at their houses and we made our way to the party on Summit. We pulled up to the house and knocked. I was shocked to see that the guy answering the door was a schoolmate of mine from grade school, Steve Bohrer. He went to Saint Thomas, so I hadn't seen him in four years.

"Steve?" I asked.

"Jim Landwehr?" he answered.

"Wow, I didn't know you guys lived on Summit."

"Yeah. C'mon in," he said.

We went downstairs where there were half a dozen couples sitting around. The stereo played top forty hits softly in the background. The room was decorated in Summit Avenue mansion splendor. Steve was a Tommie, a school that was an echelon above Cretin in terms of tuition and suburban accessibility, so it made sense he lived on Summit. It was where the other half lived.

After we settled in and made introductions to all the other couples, none of whom I knew, Steve offered me a beer. I was a little surprised to see alcohol available at a high school post dance party, but took one anyway, as did Michelle. I'm unsure whether Steve's parents were home or not, but these were different times to be sure. Over time, the party broke off into a couple of different groups each having separate conversations. Like any situation where I didn't know many people, the time spent at the gathering pushed my comfort level. I hated making small talk, but also recognized these kinds of social situations were part of growing up. While I'd much rather be with my good friends, these types of interactions make a teen more socially adept. They require listening, response and engagement with strangers. In my case, I was faking it to make it.

We talked and laughed and had a couple of beers over the course of an hour and a half before Michelle mentioned we should get going. We got up, thanked Steve and made our way to the door. I drove with a little extra caution given the beers I'd had. It was strange being alone again with Michelle. This time in the car our conversation seemed much more relaxed and natural. Perhaps it was the beer. Or, maybe it was the realization that an otherwise difficult night was coming to an end and we could go about our separate lives again. The pressure was off.

It was probably the beer.

I pulled into her driveway, we got out of the car and walked to her door.

"Well, thank you. It was nice meeting you," she said as she half-hugged me.

"Yes, it was fun," I lied.

"I'll try and get the pictures to you, sometime."

"Hey, yeah, that'd be good."

To be honest, I'm still waiting for those pictures. I guess no one needs reminders of a relatively awkward evening, but I thought it would have shown a hint of gracious class despite all we'd been through that night. I guess I still need to get over it.

As crappy as that evening was, it was a good lesson in the ups and downs of the dating life. Sometimes young people connect. Sometimes they don't. It was proof you can be a perfect gentleman – even despite the snowbank debacle – and it still doesn't guarantee that a woman will like you. Relationships are hard to establish and blind dates might be one of the worst ways to go about trying to build one. Throwing another couple into the mix doesn't necessarily help. In any case, mine was a match that was not meant to be.

CHAPTER 19: "OD"

One of the obligations of being promoted to the rank of officer at school was a requirement to serve on occasion as Officer of the Day. The position was nicknamed, "OD" and, of course, the obvious drug reference made for lots of jokes among both druggies and non-druggies alike. It was a rotating requirement assigned to all officers alphabetically, as needed. Fulfilling the post granted the officer an exemption from attending classes so they could go from room to room, collecting attendance slips from the teachers. If students were truant, they were noted on the slips. These were then reviewed by the administrative offices and follow-up disciplinary action was taken, if needed.

The OD was also tasked with raising and lowering the flag out in front of the school at the beginning and end of the school day. The obligation sounds much more glamorous than it really was. It was mostly an exercise in ensuring the flag didn't hit the ground at any point, which would be considered a desecration of Old Glory. At the daily flag raising, no taps were played, no twenty one gun salute. Just you and some other officer unfurling and hoisting away.

Personally being OD was highly coveted for me. Anytime I could get an exemption from going to classes, it was looked at as a good thing. It was a little like the simple pleasure of having an "out of uniform pass." When you are in a rigid, militaristic environment from day to day, anything outside the realm of rules or routine is a welcome change. So, on the afternoon of my OD duty, I went happily about my duties. I stopped at each room and said, "OD?" and the teachers usually waved me along. Then, I'd go on to the next until I had covered both floors in both buildings.

During fifth hour of one of my OD assignments, I had to go to the restroom. At the time, smoking in the bathrooms was a fairly common practice, despite being against the rules. I never smoked cigarettes in high school, but a few of the bolder guys did partake, both on and off

150

campus. Being prohibited only pushed it to the bathrooms and the hidden nooks and crannies of the school. I was always a bit shocked guys would be brave enough to light up in the bathroom, but they did. It seems every time I had to use the restroom there was either a fresh cloud of smoke or the faint smell of a recent cigarette. I don't know firsthand the struggles of a nic-fit, but I figure it must be pretty strong to push people to smoking in a toilet stall.

As I entered the men's room, I was not surprised by the cloud of secondhand smoke. Thinking nothing of it, I went into one of the stalls and went about my business. I washed up and was on my way toward the door when in came Brother John, my typing instructor with his crutches. As he tottered past me he said, "Hmmm, smoking in the lavatory, Mr. Landwehr?"

I was aghast. Why would he assume it was me? Couldn't he see I was on duty as OD? Would I risk doing something as stupid as smoking while making the rounds? Surely not.

Assuming he was joking, I laughed and said, "Huh, yeah right?"

He raised his eyebrows and replied with, "Hmm?" He clearly did not share my humor at the absurdity of such a false assumption. I could tell by his expression he really thought I'd done it. This was such an affront to my character. I always took pride in the fact that I didn't smoke cigarettes, so to be accused of it was something I took personally.

"No, really Brother, it wasn't me. I don't smoke!"

"Okay, we'll see."

It was obvious he was convinced and short of doing a pocket shakedown nothing would persuade him otherwise. So, I kept walking thinking I was wasting my time. I finished my last two hours of absentee slip pickups to round out the day. When I stopped into the administration office for my final report, Bubs Boland, the student disciplinarian at the time, stopped me. "Mr. Landwehr, you have a detention to serve, I believe?"

"What? A detention for what?"

"Brother said you were smoking in the men's room."

"Oh, my gosh. No, I told him it wasn't me. I don't smoke."

"He said it was definitely cigarette smoke, and you were in there," Bubs persisted.

"There's always smoke in the men's room. Guys do it all the time, but not me. Besides, I'm OD! Why would I do that as OD?"

"You're sure about that?"

"Absolutely sure. I don't even like cigarettes," I assured him. I neglected to tell him of my recent affinity for cigars that tasted like old socks with my friends on some of our wilder weekends.

"Well, okay. I'm going to trust you on this one. I've never seen you in here for detention, so keep your nose clean and you're free to go."

"Thanks Mr. Boland. I will. I appreciate it."

I walked away a free man, with my integrity almost intact. I don't know why I took this false character schmear so personally other than the fact I wasn't a detention kind of kid. Sure, I had my weekend after-school moments with skating on the edge of the law at times, but at school I was pretty much on my best behavior, at least with regards to major infractions like smoking and drugs. No one likes a false accusation. I was happy to be exonerated of any alleged wrongdoing.

CHAPTER 20: HOBO DAY

Like most high schools, Cretin held a variety of events every year for Homecoming week. It was a way of building school spirit resulting in a controlled frenzy of enthusiasm for the climactic varsity football game we consistently managed to lose from year to year. The freshmen had Frosh Field Day where they participated in a series of relay races and other feats of strength and endurance out on the practice football field. It pitted homerooms against one another and was overseen by a team of seniors. We were warned it was a chance for the seniors to run the freshmen ragged – a sort of induction into the school system. That rumor turned out to be entirely overblown and the event was not only harmless, but a lot of fun.

The sophomore event was Greased Football. It is exactly what it sounds like. Take a football, grease it up real good and have a game. I have no recollection of the actual event whatsoever, but I'm sure it was as fun as it sounds.

Junior year featured the Junior Ball Bash, which despite its title did not involve the need for groin protection. Rather, it consisted of a huge inflated ball that was set at midfield and then bashed by students using arms, legs and bodies to try to get it across the opponent's goal line. The ball was on the order of four feet tall and made the game a giant version of soccer with no handball fouls and certainly no headers. Highly touted by the upperclassmen who had played it before us, we looked forward to the game with great anticipation.

On game day teams lined up at midfield on opposing sides. The whistle was blown and guys started flinging themselves at the great orb as it volleyed back and forth up and down the field. Because team sizes were limited, a number of us were relegated to the sidelines to await game number two. After ten minutes of back and forth, the ball exploded and deflated. The ball had been bashed to death. It seems after years of abuse, it had taken all it could. The students stood around it looking befuddled, not sure what to do. After a brief consultation, the senior referees concluded there was no fixing it. The game was called, and that was the end of the 1977 Junior Ball Bash. Ten minutes of excitement. I think we resorted to a game of softball.

The senior year event was called Hobo Day. It was held the Friday of homecoming week and it revolved around allowing senior students to wear costumes to school. I wanted my costume to be big and over the top. The bar was set high six years earlier when my brother went dressed as a bottle of Boones Farm wine. I'd always thought that was a unique idea, if not maybe a little inappropriate for a high school setting. Stealing from his idea, I committed to constructing a life sized papier mache beer can. Part of the idea was to poke the authority structure at the school a little bit. Over four years I'd been a fairly conformant student, a relative pillar in the clique known as the straights, and I aimed to do something to change that image. I can't explain this need to appear as someone I was not, but I think it's just part of the high school experience.

After consulting with my brother, I started my project with a chicken wire frame. I conjoined two circular sections of chicken wire to make a five foot tall tube. I capped the top off with another piece and my wire exoskeleton frame was complete. I climbed into it and determined where the eye hole and arm holes needed to be cut. I cut them with a wire cutter and twisted back any sharp edges. Next I took entire sheets of newspaper, dipped them in a mixture of flour and water and wrapped the chicken wire from top to bottom. This was as messy and as drippy as it sounds. At one point the paper started to peel off because my mixture was too watery with not enough flour. I began to panic because I'd already invested a significant amount of time into the project. If I had invested as much time into my Algebra and History studies at this age I'd have been a better person, but, hey look, I'm making a huge beer can!

I adjusted the problematic area and reapplied a thicker base layer of mache. Then I let the shell dry overnight. I was relieved the next day to see the layer had adhered and I was able to move forward with the project. I applied a second layer and again let it dry. When my friends started asking what I was planning for Hobo Day, I told them I was going as a beer can and it was going to be awesome. At the time, I hadn't thought far enough ahead about how I would transport the behemoth costume to and from school, but first things first.

When the shell was done it was time for the fun part, the paint. My original plan was to try to re-create the popular favorite beer brand of the time, Miller High Life. Again, my lack of foresight came back to bite me when I looked at the label design for a can. Between the ornate fonts, and all the putzy artistry that obviously went into the Miller branding, it would clearly take a hand more artistic than my own to pull this one off. It would also require four different colors of both spray and brush-on paint. My budget was about to blow up. Between the expense and the concern that I didn't have the artistic flair for some of the lettering, I had to rethink my strategy.

At the time, I collected beer cans and displayed them above the woodwork around the door and windows of my bedroom. To find a suitable replacement logo, I scanned my beer can collection, for a simpler label that a graphic design-challenged teenager could actually replicate. The label that seemed the easiest to re-create was for Red White and Blue beer. I'd never tasted a Red White and Blue, but my brother Tom mentioned it was basically the bottom of the barrel for the Pabst lineup of beers. In a word, it was rotgut.

So here I was, constructing a costume of a product I'd never consumed simply because it was easier. Makes perfect sense.

I purchased the paint I thought I needed and set to work on the base coat. The white did a poor job of covering the newsprint. After I'd emptied a can of white spray paint and barely covered one half the costume, I realized I was going to need a whole lot more paint before things were done. This project was killing me! I began to wonder why I didn't just go to Hobo Day as a pirate or something? Or, better yet, a hobo. Now there was a concept! Holey jeans, flannel shirt, bandana on a stick. Done.

At this point though, I was in deep. I needed to finish the project. I'd begun to hate the whole idea, but was determined to finish it out. A trip to the hardware store to get more paint and I was on my way. I finished the base coat in a cloud of toxic aerosol and then moved on to the hand painted portion. The lettering was a simple font even an artistic hack could replicate. When the lettering was done, I added the diagonal blue and red ribbons and a few other details and called it done. Then, I cut a bicycle tire inner tube into two pieces and strung them from the inside to be worn like suspenders holding the whole unwieldy contraption in place. I climbed into the beer can again - which seems like a metaphor for my later years as a twenty something – and after a couple of adjustments to the suspenders, I had myself a real, live beer can body. It bobbed and bounced a little more than I liked because of the nature of the rubber suspenders, but it was much too late in the game at that point to make any adjustments. I'd have to live with it.

Now the question arose, how would I get it transported to school? On the Thursday of homecoming week I asked Pete if we could haul it in his dad's Cadillac Coupe de Ville convertible. He said he could pick up both Pat and me. We'd be a bunch of hobos travelling in style, that's for sure.

Friday morning came around and Pete showed up at my house with Pat in the passenger seat. He sounded his old-timey ahhoogah horn. I wrestled the giant can off my porch, down the steps and set it in the back seat of the Caddy. I sat next to it and held onto it as Pete pulled out onto Lexington Parkway.

Now, I've seen a lot of strange things going down the roadway in my day. Women applying makeup on the freeway, people holding mattresses on the roof of a sedan with hands out the windows and people steering with their knees while eating a hamburger. But outside of my own experience, I've never seen three teenagers in a Cadillac convertible cruising at thirty with a six foot beer can in the back seat. You just can't make that stuff up, you have to live it. And there we were, a spectacle to behold.

After our fifteen minute, one float alcoholic parade to school, Pete dropped me off at the front door. I pulled my can on and headed up the front steps. Steps were an obstacle I hadn't given much thought to. I ended up lifting the can a little, like a woman might lift her dress, to get up them unimpeded. It took a little getting used to, but the rubber suspenders I had on the inside actually made things easy enough.

It was when I got into the hallways of the school that things got interesting. Random guys took abnormal delight in taking pot shots at the can from behind or as they passed. Because I had essentially a single porthole to see out of, by the time I turned my head to see who had whacked me, they had already blended into the crowd of other students. It's the same kind of behavior taken out on mascots at sporting events. Evidently there's something irresistible about a person wearing an oversized anything that makes people want to hit it. This probably stems from the indefensibility of the outfit. I was like Godzilla out there, swinging my arms helplessly and constantly taking fire from those pesky little fighter jets.

I walked down the hall drawing laughs and high fives from students from all grade levels. I was a beer can hero. Mama would be so proud! When I came to the steps up to the second floor I again had to navigate them carefully, lift, step, lift, step. Fortunately, teachers were a little more laid back with the seniors on this day, so if I were late to class because of my costume I would at least be granted a little grace.

When I got to my homeroom, Mr. Hughes greeted me with a dropped jaw. He wasn't sure what to think of the "quiet kid," Jim Landwehr, coming to school dressed up as an alcoholic beverage. To be honest, shock was a bit of my intent. After being the good kid for four years, I was ready to change my image. It may have been a bit of a poke at the administration of oppression as well. At Cretin we had both the Church and State kind of keeping us down – both things we signed up for when we chose it as our school, I fully realize. But sometimes it felt good to poke the beast. This was my artistic freedom of speech coming out, and while it may have been a tad inappropriate in a high school setting, there wasn't much that could be done about it. It's my guess subsequent classes at Cretin had to adhere to some sort of Hobo Day costume appropriateness policy. I wouldn't blame the administration if there was.

The rest of the morning was spent going from class to class. It involved getting my costume on, walking to class, taking shots to the midsection along the way, and then stepping out of the can so I could sit at my desk. Change classes, and repeat. I won't lie, after the third class period, the whole routine got kind of old. The chicken wire was starting to scratch my arms in a few places and the novelty was beginning to wane.

The last couple periods of Senior Hobo Day were given to the seniors to spend walking from classroom to classroom and drumming up school spirit for the homecoming football game later that evening. I was part of a large pack of seniors who roamed the halls disrupting classes one at a time. We walked into room after room led by Billy Walsh, Tim Godfrey and John Mueller. These guys were all big on school spirit. In each room they took turns announcing to all the underclassmen we were going to sing the Cretin Rouser, and everyone needed to participate. Then, we'd all sing the rouser with gusto.

Oh dear Cretin High, the greatest school in all the land.
Our Alma Mater we doff our hats to thee and stand.
The purple and gold spells loyalty we're proud to show.

Hail Cretin, Rah! Rah! Hoo-Rah! Hail Cretin High let's go!
Fair school of our youth, our happiest days were spent with thee.
The friendships we've made, will live fore'er in memory.
Wherever we go our motto always VICTORY.
Hail Cretin, Rah! Rah! Hoo-Rah! Hail Cretin High let's go!

Having been on the receiving end for three years as an underclassman, it felt good being among the costumed ones dishing out the directive for a change. Hobo Day was one of those high school days I will always remember. I enjoyed school events and saw things like this as a last chance to celebrate my days as a high schooler. I was taking part in a tradition that had been around for generations, and training up the next class in how it was done. It felt good to be king for a day.

The last bell rang signaling the end of the day. I put on my can for the last time and met my friends by the back doors of the main building. When I saw Pete, I said, "Hey, can you give me and my can a ride home?"

"You aren't really going to keep that are you?"

"Uh, I was thinking about it," I replied.

"What are you going to do with it?"

I hadn't really thought about that, but Pete had a good point. It had served its purpose and I was hard pressed to think of another possible use for it.

"Well, what should I do with it?" I asked.

"There's a dumpster right over there. Why don't you pitch it?"

Given all the work I put into making the costume, it seemed odd to just discard it after only six hours of use. But I was also ready to be relieved of the confines of my chicken wire punching bag. I walked over to the dumpster, took off the can and heaved it in. I had to admit, it was a little liberating. I walked back to his dad's car and climbed in. We were one costume less than when we'd started, but it had been a good day. Pete switched on the radio and the three of us hoboes rode his Cadillac Coupe De Ville away from the school.

CHAPTER 21: TWILIGHT

Cretin hosted a public event every spring called Twilight Parade, or as we students referred to it, simply, "Twilight." The parade was held in May a few weeks before school let out. It was an effort to allow parents, family and friends to come watch their boys and perhaps witness a bit of a return on their tuition investment. The boys marched in full dress uniform from the practice football field on the south of campus to the track and field area on the north side. Once there, the ranks formed up and listened to military staff teachers give speeches and student achievement recognitions.

As seniors, this event marked the last parade we were required to show in. But as the outgoing upperclassmen, we were also expected to be on our best behavior, role models for the younger guys. This didn't stop the guys in the party crowd from using it as a chance to have a few covert beers before or afterward to help make the whole thing more bearable. Threats were issued every year that any students caught or suspected of drinking would be pulled from the parade. Though I never drank before the event, the threat of being pulled actually appealed to me as it would mean not having to suffer through the hour and a half ordeal.

The ranks formed up on south field. Squads into platoons, platoons into companies, companies into a brigade. Looking back, I can't imagine trying to get that number of adolescent boys to form anything more than an unruly mob with attention issues, but somehow it was pulled off year after year. Once the rows and columns were brought to attention, the snare and bass drums started drumming to mark time. Then the company commander shouted, "Alpha Company, forward march!" At this, the Bravo and Charlie company commanders countered, "Stand fast!" to remind their companies to wait their turn.

When my company was called we started marching in place until the whole mass of adolescent humanity began to move. Of course there was always a smattering of guys hopping at the beginning of the drumming while they got the rhythm. During the march everyone was fairly focused and quiet, but without fail, every year there was the occasional wise cracking student who would utter one liners and get the whole squad tittering. It was never audible to the watching crowd, but it was proof despite the appearance of the highest level of military professionalism, we were really just a bunch of half-invested teens clomping toward adulthood.

After a five minute march to north field, we formed up again in neat rows. We shifted between standing at attention and "resting" at parade rest as directed by the commanding officers. Prior to the parade we were reminded to not lock our knees when standing at attention. The claim was that it cut off the blood flow to other critical parts of our bodies, most notably, our heads, and caused fainting. It was an annual warning for Twilight, but every year a fainting or two seemed to happen despite the warnings.

Well, this year was no different. Thirty minutes into the presentation ceremonies, as I stood there at attention, I turned to my left to see a guy one platoon over fall face first like a logged tree. There was never any breaking of the fall with these poor fellows. One minute they're stick straight, and the next, a corpse inspecting the grass at close range. Man down!

The platoon leader quickly went to the guy's aid. He turned the cadet over, loosened the necktie, patted him on the cheek and tried to revive the poor guy. After a minute the student was sitting up wondering what hit him. One thing is for sure, it would be embarrassing having to explain the grass stains on the knees of his pants when he got home.

When the speeches and recognitions were all done, we were called to march past the review stand. This meant passing in front of Colonel Fahs, Colonel Maher and the student cadet colonel, Larry McCallum. At the command, "Eyes left" we turned our heads toward the viewing stand and continued marching. After we passed, the command "Ready, front!" was issued and we swiveled our heads back to front. Of course, as boys do, we adapted the phrase eyes right, or eyes left to social situations whenever a cute Derham Hall girl was anywhere near. In that respect, our military training taught us some skills besides the maximum effective range of an M16. Attractive girl code-speak.

Twilight Parade marked the end of the school year and was a swan song for the seniors. To those of us graduating the following month, it was our march toward the future. In some ways it felt good to get it out of the way and coast into graduation. But in other ways it was a sort of sad occasion. It was the beginning of the end of our high school experience. What made Cretin unique was its JROTC program, so this was also essentially our release from our military service. Some guys went on to military pursuits in college or the armed forces, but for most of us we would never have to shine brass or wear our hair short again. And while that was absolutely freeing, part of me acknowledges I learned much about discipline and respect via the codes and requirements of time spent in a military uniform. The discipline alone provided me with a life skill for my future. And if I ever needed it, I was fully capable of putting a good spit shine on a pair of shoes.

CHAPTER 22: GRADUATION

Senior graduation was held at Saint Catherine's University, a short distance down Randolph Avenue from the Cretin campus. Our school auditorium was too small for the event, so they held it at St. Kate's every year. Staying true to Cretin's military roots and traditions, students didn't wear the customary cap and gown. We wore our school military garb, including our drab green caps, white gloves and dress blouses. The ceremony was carried out with all the pomp and circumstance of any graduation.

After the initial introduction and class prayer, Greg Kiwus took the podium and gave an inspiring speech as class valedictorian. His speech ended with a reference to the Rolling Stones song, "You Can't Always Get What You Want." It was met with rousing applause. Everybody liked Greg and respected his smarts. His address was followed by one by my homeroom teacher, Mr. Hughes. The Class of '79 marked his first class he'd taken through four years together as a new teacher at Cretin, so it was an especially proud moment for him. Afterward, he wowed the crowd with a couple of his magic tricks.

I took my moment of walking across the stage and shaking hands with the administrators as part of what was a normal commencement. It came with the requisite hat toss and chaotic parental photo session on the lawn following. With the official send-off over, the evening set in and brought a more exciting twist to the festive occasion.

Word travelled between my friends that Paul Flynn was having a party at his parent's house on Summit Avenue. Rumor had it his parents weren't home and there was going to be a keg of beer and a bunch of people. Pete, Pat, Dan, and I all knew Paul, but none of us were great friends with him. We all knew, because this was graduation, we would probably never see some of these guys again, so it seemed like it was worth a shot. It beat staying home on one of the biggest days of our young lives and the worst they could do was turn us away at the door.

We showed up around 7:30 PM and after paying a few bucks, were each given a cup and pointed in the direction of the keg in the garage area out back. The June evening air was warm and humid as the four of us headed toward the beer and filled our cups. There were a number of familiar faces we had all seen around the halls at school. Guys we didn't really associate with over senior year, or any year for that matter, who suddenly became chummy with us. People were relaxed and the mere presence of a keg levelled the playing field for all of us men-boys. Our mingling was aided by a few go-betweens, the easy-going guys everyone in the school seemed to like. Guys like Bill Robertson, a sports junkie who aspired to be a sportscaster. He always called me Alan Landwehr after a baseball player of the same name. It was an endearing trait from a guy who just loved people, and was out to prove it. These types of guys were the ones at parties like this who made everyone feel comfortable.

Rock music thumped in the background as we stood talking and laughing in a circle like most every keg party that ever happened. Classmates drifted in and out of the circle which grew and shrunk with each coming and going. Talk ranged from what our plans were for the future, to favorite memories of our days at Cretin, to teachers we would and wouldn't miss. When that grew old, we talked about movies and our favorite bands. No one was saying it, but this party signaled a transition in all of our friendships none of us could avoid. Most of us were off to college in the fall and that brought with it a new set of responsibilities. Time together would become more difficult to come by, and the friendships we once took for granted would now require intentionality and effort to sustain. So we relished these moments of camaraderie, as Cretin Raiders together, for at least one more night, and drank our cheap American pilsner.

After an hour or so, an older couple walked into the backyard. All eyes turned to Paul, who seemed suddenly very concerned about the apparently unexpected visit. He approached the couple and, after a short exchange, followed them into the house. Our circle of revelers exchanged worrisome glances between one another.

"That can't be good," Pat said.

"Yeah, looks like the parental units," Pete added.

"Well, this was fun while it lasted," Dan chimed in.

After a few minutes, Paul came out of the house with an announcement. "The bad news is, this party is over. The good news is, you guys can take the keg and move the party elsewhere," he said.

The four of us agreed moving the party, rather than killing it, was good news. It was still early, barely eight o'clock. A few of the guys convened and strategized a new location where the kegger could continue. Word eventually got around that the party was being moved to the Saint Paul Academy soccer field, a high school located down the street from Cretin. For some reason, the idea of moving the keg to a private grounds to trespass in full view of the world seemed like a perfectly logical idea to our not-fully developed teenaged frontal lobes. What could possibly go wrong?

We finished up our beers and piled into Dan's truck. He worked his way toward Saint Paul Academy as we rehashed the conversations we had back at Paul's house with our classmates. When we got to the soccer field we were surprised to see there was already a dozen people gathered around the keg. These guys really knew how to move a party. We walked to midfield and joined the celebration in progress. On arrival, we were greeted by Kevin Galligan, one of the most popular guys in our class. "To the new arrivals!" Kevin shouted and raised his plastic cup.

"To the new arrivals!" the crowd echoed. In unison the small crowd raised their cups.

Everyone took a drink and continued with their conversations. Not wanting to miss out, we each grabbed a cup and made our way to the beer. It was uncertain as to how long this party would go before we were forced to move again or how long the keg would last, so we figured we had better drink while the drinking was good.

Before long, the novelty of Kevin's toast generated another. Billy Walsh raised his glass and said, "To the class of '79!"

The crowd echoed, "To the class of '79!" a cheer went up and everyone took a swig. It seemed to catch on as yet another guy offered a toast, "To Brother Pius! Long live Brother Pius!"

"Long live Brother Pius!" another cheer as we all toasted again. The toasting became the main event. It went around the crowd featuring a different guy each time. When my turn came, I shouted, "To Mrs. Bean's bean burgers!" referencing the questionable meat-to-soybean ratio in her alleged hamburgers.

"To Mrs. Bean!"

After more revelry and a couple more toasts, a pair of headlights flicked on behind the fencing on the far end of the field. Then, another pair illuminated from another direction. Then, a third. We all swiveled our heads in the direction of each set as they came on. Assessing the situation with a barley infused sense of humor, Kevin offered up a spontaneous, parting toast.

"To...the cops are here!"

The crowd raised their glasses for a final toast, "The cops are here!"

Everyone took a last swig and scattered like cockroaches in every direction. A few even shouted the line from the movie *Monty Python and The Holy Grail*, "Runaway! Runaway!"

I threw my cup down and broke into a full sprint in the opposite direction of the oncoming headlights. The party was a blast while it happened, but the last way I wanted to end it was in the back of a squad car or, worse, in jail. I hauled ass across the field until I came to a six-foot cyclone fence. It was intended to keep riff-raff like us off the premises and now it was keeping us in. Without a thought, I jumped onto it and started to Spiderman my way over the top. I clawed my way up like a convict on the lam.

Nearly out of breath, I heaved my body over the top, managing to snag my shirt on the top of the fence in the process, tearing a small hole. "Aw, crap!" I said, as I continued my way down the backside of the fence. It was a small enough hole it wasn't likely to generate too many questions should Mom come across it, but it was also one of my favorite shirts. At the moment my adrenaline rush was preventing me from worrying about repercussions for it. A torn shirt would be easier to explain than asking Mom to post bail.

Halfway down the backside of the fence I let go and dropped to the ground. I took off running and made my way into the relative darkness of the school grounds. I never looked back to see if the cops had fanned out to chase us, but wasn't about to stick around to find out. Seeking cover, I ran toward a huge pine tree with low hanging boughs. I crawled under the lowest branches, which hung to the ground, and lay there trying to catch my breath. My heart pounded wildly in my chest. I'd never run from the cops and it was proving to be both frightening, and exhilarating, at the same time. I didn't plan on making it a regular occurrence, but neither did I plan to get caught on this occasion.

I lay there a good fifteen minutes before it appeared safe enough to come out from my cover. Standing up, I brushed myself free of pine needles and dirt and tried my best to look nonchalant as I walked away. I'm sure it looked shady as heck to any passerby that might have witnessed it. A tall, gangly teenager crawling out from under a tree after dark like some sort of gigantic Hobbit-Troll. Yeah, it happens all the time.

I stealthed across the school grounds to the sidewalk and headed toward Cleveland Avenue to make my way home, about three miles away. Once I got to Cleveland, I walked for a block and then turned down a side street, reasoning that if the cops were looking for suspicious teenagers, they'd stick to the main streets. Slinking down each street, I walked briskly, trying to look guilt free despite having beer breath and a torn shirt. *Nothing to see here officer, nothing at all.* I kept my eyes peeled for Dan's car on the off chance he was out looking for those of us who had ridden with him to the kegger. I guessed that like the rest of us, he'd taken the route of "every man for himself," and was driving straight home alone.

After an hour's walk, I arrived home. As luck would have it, Mom was out for the evening, so I didn't have to report to anyone.

Graduation night will forever live in my mind as the last big adventure and near miss of my high school years at Cretin. My classmates and I went out with a bang, bonded our friendship one last time, and narrowly avoided arrest in the process. During our celebratory toasts on the field that night, we all put our differences aside and celebrated our collectiveness. No one knew where our future journeys would take us, though we'd all travelled down the same path to get here. Whether you were a geek, a jock, a brain, a straight, or a burn out, it didn't matter. That particular night we were all on the same team celebrating our accomplishments and turning to face tomorrow's world. And we all knew that, forevermore, we would be Raiders!

CHAPTER 23: 30TH REUNION

In 1986, two years after my five year reunion, I moved to Wisconsin. I took a job there after getting laid off from a mapping job in Minneapolis. I essentially set out on my own and started my life over. Despite getting class reunion notices every five years, the thought of going back to the Twin Cities for a high school reunion just didn't seem attractive. When the thirtieth reunion rolled around, my thoughts shifted and I ruminated about making an effort to attend. The 30 number seemed so different, more significant in some way. Could it really have been thirty years? It seemed impossible, and yet there I was, in the throes of middle age a state away with a wife and two children, wondering if any of my core group of friends were feeling drawn to reconnecting after so long.

I hadn't really been in touch with anyone from Cretin since my five year reunion except occasional contact with a couple of my closer friends. The reunion notice read that the festivities would take place in the courtyard of Cretin-Derham. It was the name they took after merging with Derham Hall in 1987 to become a coed high school. I hadn't been back in the building since I graduated thirty years prior and, being a hopeless nostalgic, I thought it would be a cool walk back into my past.

So I checked with Pat, Pete and Dan to see if they would be going. Pete was living in Baltimore, but said it would be nice to get together and agreed to travel to make it happen. After living in Oklahoma for several years, Pat moved back to Lakeville, Minnesota, a bedroom community of Minneapolis. Now that he was local, he also agreed he would be interested. When I contacted Dan via social media, he politely declined the offer, saying he wasn't big on group gatherings and didn't have much of a desire to go back. I could certainly respect that. When I asked everyone about Doug, most said they'd either not heard from him or that he seemed kind of distant or aloof when they ran into him in public. No one was quite sure why he made such an attempt to standoff from all of us, but I guess sometimes people want to erase their prior selves and move on. It wouldn't stop the rest of us from trying to reconnect with one another, but neither would we persist and try to make him do something he had no interest in. He was a good friend in high school and that was enough for everyone, I guess. To each his own.

***

The Class of '79 thirty-year reunion was to be a two-day affair with an evening social at the school on Friday, followed by a golf outing on Saturday morning and a social gathering at Costello's bar that night. Mike Costello was a classmate who owned and operated a bar in Saint Paul and offered to host.

Pat, Pete and I agreed in advance we would all attend the Friday stag social at the school and the joint Cretin High, Derham Hall cocktail outing at Costello's on Saturday. None of our wives had interest in any part of it. I can't blame them. I'd feel the same had my wife ever attended any of her reunions. (She hasn't!) We also decided we would skip the large class-wide group golf outing on Saturday and golf on our own. After all, our intent was mainly to get back in touch with each other, and a round of golf with just the three of us would provide lots of time for that.

Surreal is the only way to describe how it felt when I arrived and walked alone up those front steps and into the school again. It had been thirty years and a few weeks since I'd left the school and I had nary stepped foot in the place since. Sometimes you close a book and don't open it for a long time. Such was the case with old "Dear Cretin High, greatest school in all the land," words taken from our school song. It may have been for some of the students in my class, but for me, it was just a required stop on the road to higher things. It gave me a decent education that provided a jump start to college, and a career after that. Those days in the late '70s were good, but if anyone asked, it wasn't a time I'd particularly want to go back to. High school years are a distant second best to those spent in college in my opinion. But after three decades, I thought a visit back was in order.

I walked in the front door and looked up to see the big framed pictures of the previous graduating classes still hanging in the main hallway near the front office. My stepfather's picture was there among the '40s somewhere. My stepbrothers, my brother Tom's and my own fell in the '70s group. It felt good to know those class photos that were hanging there back in my day, were still important enough to warrant a little wall space in 2009. It gave recognition and credence to those who'd gone before. It was our school's pictorial history.

I wandered back to the doorway leading to the outdoor courtyard, a large square of greenery on the ground level. Shrubs, flowers and a couple of statues lined the perimeter of the large open lawn with pathways zig-zagging across it. In one corner stood a table with stainless serving pans warmed by lit cans of Sterno flaming beneath them. Hamburgers and hot dogs, chips and accompaniments were the menu for the evening. The casual setting featured a half dozen standing tables with small groups of guys milling around them.

I checked in at the registration table. Kevin Galligan, who I hadn't seen since that fateful night around the keg on the soccer field, was manning the table and greeted me, crossing my name off the list of registrants. He was still one of those genuine people who knew almost everyone in the class, and, even more astounding, didn't forget them over the years.

After I registered, I spotted Pete talking to Pat at one of the tables, so I sauntered over. Time hadn't been kind to either of our hairlines, but otherwise he looked much the same as I remembered. Pat, who was always wiry and gangly in high school, had put on some weight, but actually wore it pretty well. I gave each of them a man hug, not too long, but one that reminded us of the days we had together years before.

"So, how you guys doing?" I asked.

"Doing well, and how about you?" Pat asked. He was always more interested in hearing about others than talking about himself. I always admired his humility and interest in people and their lives. After an update from me and Pete about our jobs, wives and kids, he talked about his own family and described some of his experiences as a police chaplain for the City of Saint Paul. I listened with keen interest as he went on about some of the tough situations he dealt with in his role. Death notifications to parents of children were some of the hardest, he said. Pat was in the publishing business by day, but volunteered as a chaplain on the side. He had a deep faith and lived it out in many ways, this being perhaps the biggest manifestation of it.

We talked and ate as guys wandered into the courtyard, some looking familiar, some not. Tom Gautschi walked up. Tom was another one of the good guys most everyone at school liked. He was always on the inner fringe of our friend group, so we spent some time catching up with him. His career was in trucking and it was funny how the core of his personality was still the same, a great sense of humor, an easygoing personality and quick with a laugh. It was pretty true for all of us. In high school, the clay is wet, and we spend the rest of our lives spinning and shaping ourselves until we are fully formed.

After an hour or so, I excused myself and went inside to the men's room. While I was in there a couple of guys were chatting. When they saw me, they introduced themselves and asked my name. I told them, and they confessed that out in the courtyard they and others were wondering who the tall guy in the red shirt was. They also admitted they didn't remember me being as tall as I was. Having been absent from reunions for the past twenty-five years, I guess I could understand how they might not recognize me. It was also a testament to my high school years where I fell among the many "average" B-students whose presence outside their core friend groups was fairly anonymous and forgettable. I was okay both then and now with my anonymous and forgettable persona. As a self-diagnosed introvert, anonymous was good. Blending in was an quality to aspire to.

A light rain began shortly after I returned from the men's room. It cut the discussions short and forced guys into the hallway. We were told to move to the auditorium for a class picture and an ad-hoc magic show by my old homeroom teacher, Hondo Hughes. As we collectively filed toward the auditorium, John Cooper, a feisty guy who had too much to drink found it necessary to express his political opinions to Chris Coleman, a '79er who was the current Mayor of Saint Paul.

"I don't like you, or your politics!" he said, swaying and sloshing at arm's length from Chris. Mayor Coleman did his best to defuse the drunk alumni. Like the mayor or not -I did-, no one could deny the fact that one of our own was a powerful political leader and he deserved more respect than the inebriated one was giving him. To his credit, Chris chose not to engage and eventually the instigator was distracted by others trying to defuse the situation. It made for an uncomfortable few minutes and was more like high school than any of us would like to admit. Some guys grow up faster than others, I guess.

Hondo took the stage in front of us. He hadn't taught at Cretin for a few decades, yet made it a point to show up for the reunion of the first graduating class he saw start-to-finish. He started by saying a few words about how this class was his first as a new teacher. It was a heartfelt recognition of how far we had all come. He then wowed and amazed us with his expert sleight-of-hand, just as he had in those moments in high school when he'd take time to show us a new trick he'd been practicing. He hadn't lost a step.

When he was done, he took a couple of photos of our class in the stadium seating of the auditorium. We filed out and many of us began making our way toward the exit. It had been an enjoyable evening of looking back, retracing old steps and stories and bringing one another up to speed on where life had taken us since we'd seen each other last. It was about what I expected after being away for a quarter of a century. I was actually looking forward to catching up a bit more the following day with my old friends, both close and not so close.

***

Pete, Pat and I teed off early on Saturday morning at Highland Golf Course, just down Hamline Avenue from Cretin. Time had not sharpened my game at all since the days when my golf bag weighed more than me. My slices, hooks and whiffs were sprinkled among the occasional shots that kept my confidence up. The frustrating thing about the game is that just when you think you're the worst player in the world, you land a perfect shot or drive the ball a mile. It's these moments of athletic personal heroism that keep me coming back to the game, like a dog to its vomit.

On the second or third hole, Pat broke out three fat cigars. Nothing goes better with a slow moving, highly difficult game than a fine stogie. These smokes were considerable upgrades from the Swisher Sweets we shared as friends in the caves of thirty-plus years ago. The habit had stuck with all three of us at different levels, me when fishing, and Pete and Pat in social situations while enjoying a cocktail. We fired them up and resumed our game. There we were, looking like a bunch of rich fat cats on the course, even though our vehicles and mortgages proved otherwise.

After we finished our round, Pat said, "You guys up for a couple beers?"

"Sure am. Let's go to the Nook, across the street from school," Pete said.

"That'll work. Nice and close," I said.

We drove to the bar only to find it was packed, and loud. Since we wanted to talk and catch up, we agreed this place wasn't going to work.

"We could pick up some beer at the liquor store across the street and drink it somewhere," Pat said. He was always the edgy one of the group, prone to moments of spontaneity and recklessness. Apparently those tendencies still held true. We crossed the street, went into the liquor store and picked up a six-pack.

"Where we going to drink these, out of a paper bag at the bus stop?" I joked.

Pat and Pete cracked up.

"How about the park across from the golf course? They have a park there," Pete suggested. Sure, the cops would never think to look for illicit drinkers in a park, I thought, sarcastically. In any case, it would be better than a bus stop, so I agreed it was a wiser choice.

We drove to the park, and found a picnic table to sit around. I wasn't sure, but I thought we were within a stone's throw from the Valley where our encounter with the law happened that fateful night in '79. I also knew that drinking alcohol in a public park was *still* illegal, so I was fairly uneasy as we sat, and popped the caps on our first beer. Pete offered Pat and me a cigar which we both accepted. We clinked our bottles together, and said "To thirty years!" and took a swig. It was a cheer not unlike the one we'd had on the soccer field on graduation night thirty years earlier.

And we sat there for an hour, puffing, swilling our beer and laughing *exactly* as we had when we all struggled with acne, grades and girl problems. The conversation went from topic to topic as we tried to catch each other up with where our lives had taken us. Wives, kids, jobs, houses, dogs and hobbies. None of us tried to one-up one another. Each of us had experienced our own successes and struggles and we talked about them to the level we were comfortable. There were stories about our Cretin days mixed in for sure, but largely we talked about what we'd done after the days in those halls.

Pat was the one who pointed out that despite being thirty years later, we were almost in the exact same situation, drinking beer, smoking stogies and laughing our heads off within walking distance of the Cretin-Derham campus. It was a moment I will remember forever

– time spent with guys I literally had not seen in years. Yet here we were picking up where we left off, barely missing a step. That kind of comfort, ease and assurance is how you differentiate the lifelong friends from the ones that are part of your life for a few years and then, for whatever reason, they fade.

We hung out for an hour, drank a couple of beers and renewed our longstanding friendship. Unlike those brushes with the law in '79, the cops never showed up at this spontaneous cocktail hour, and, as nervous as I was, it sure felt good to be among a couple of old friends.

***

I arrived at Costello's bar about fifteen minutes after the Saturday social started the next evening. Many of my classmates were still at the golf event and hadn't arrived yet. I looked around and Pat and Pete were nowhere to be seen. These sorts of situations are my personal nightmare. I sensed I would be pressed into social situations to make small talk with people I hadn't seen in thirty years, a perfect storm for those of us with threads of socially anxiety. The weather was pleasant and they had some outside seating, so I sat down at a table with Josh Daniels. Josh was a classmate at both Cretin and Saint Luke's, my grade school before that.

"Hey, Jim Landwehr, how you doing?" he said.

"I'm good, how about you, Josh?" I asked.

We went on for a few minutes small talking and filling the silence with words. Josh was always the cool, popular, good looking kid and never had much time for quiet guys like me. I remember thinking it was nice he was engaging and making an effort to converse, but we both sort of knew that we were just killing time until the people we wanted to hang around with showed up. I guess that is a realization probably shared by many. Perhaps high school reunions are not supposed to be anything more than that – a reconnection of the ones who matter and small talk with the rest. Understand, it's not that the reconnection with some of the people you knew as an adolescent wasn't of some value, because it was. It's just not the best part of what the past couple of days had given me.

After a few minutes Pat and Pete arrived. I excused myself and went inside the bar with them. The three of us ordered beers and gathered around a table. Hors de oeuvres warmed on a table in the back as people wandered in and out of the bar. As I looked around the room, I marveled at how far we'd all come. Thirty years ago most of us had no idea where we would end up. Some, like Pete, would join the military service and move on to become successful attorneys. Others, like myself and Pat, would follow our hunches and end up with careers we loved in mapping and Christian publishing. Still others, like Mike Costello, would end up as owners of local small businesses.

After a bit, Dave Slattery came over and started chatting with us. While Dave and I never much hung out in high school, I knew him from the grade school football team. He was another one of those guys everybody liked. His nickname was Slats and over the course of the weekend, I'd learned he was an electrician who also had been to the Boundary Waters Canoe Area several times, like myself. Dave heard I was working on a book about the area and it spurred a wonderful chat with him. He has a heart the size of Texas and seemed genuinely interested in everyone he talked to. Approachable, affable and easy to talk to, my conversation with him was a bright moment in the evening. We caught up with our family lives and swapped a few stories as we sipped our beers.

A little later, Margaret McElhatton stopped by our table. As I mentioned, the social at Costellos was a mixed school event with the Derham Hall class of '79. She was a Derham Hall graduate who I hadn't seen since we were grade school classmates at St. Lukes. Like Slats, she was always an extremely likeable person. For someone I'd not seen in thirty four years, she still had the same great energy and upbeat personality I remembered from eighth grade. She hung out with us for a half hour and we all reminisced a bit about our days at St. Luke's, Cretin and Derham hall.

My sister Jane was having a family gathering that night so I had to leave the bar earlier than I would have liked. What I term my "closet extrovert," was in full swing and I was really enjoying the company of my past. While my days with acne, a dishwashing job and in desperate need of a girlfriend were none I wanted to return to, it was sure fun looking back. I liken it to what women say about childbirth where you forget the pain after the child is born and you fall in love with the child. High school was like that for me once I was out. I tend to romanticize it, but looking back, it was simply a portal to bigger things. While the words of the Cretin rouser, "...*our happiest days were spent with thee,*" are most certainly not true, they are offset by the following line.

The friendships we've made, will live fore'er in memory...
I certainly couldn't deny that.

EPILOGUE

I got a text from Pat in mid-July of 2018. It read:

Can I buy you Bob Seger Tickets for your bday this year? He's in town 12/12/2018. If you'll come, I'll get some.

Earlier in the summer Pat was out on his deck listening to music when Seger's song, "Like a Rock," came on the radio. He listened closely to the lyrics and later told me it was almost like a spiritual experience. The essence of the song is a middle aged narrator recounting his days as an eighteen year-old. It speaks of that period of life when we were young and strong and full of dreams.

Anyway, he texted me shortly after he heard the song and mentioned its impact. Then, after a little Googling, he found that Seger was touring and would be in the Twin Cities on December 12th, the day after my 57th birthday. We'd seen Bob Seger together in 1980, so Pat thought it would be fun to re-create the experience thirty-eight years later.

Being a sappy nostalgic, I thought it sounded like a cool idea. While I was keen on the idea of hanging out with Pat, unequivocally my best friend in high school, it was still three hundred miles from home during a busy time of year before the holidays. I told him I'd have to talk to my wife, Donna. He told me to do three things, namely, talk to Donna, pray about it, and listen to the lyrics of "Like a Rock." I told him I would do all three, but I also mentioned the only thing I could think of with that particular song was Chevy pickup commercials which used it as their jingle.

Donna and I were at a point in our lives where we'd adopted a "See-the-aging-rockstars-before-they're-dead" mentality. Rock and roll was going through a period where it was losing big stars like Prince, David Bowie and Tom Petty, just a few of the greats we'd grown up with. To squelch our fear of missing out on more, we made attempts in the past couple years to see some of the remaining, aging rockers so we could check them off our list. It was an expensive pursuit as it seemed the older these groups got, the more they charged.

When I mentioned the idea to Donna, she said I should go. "It would be a good opportunity to see your friend, and it fits with our see-the-old-rockers mantra."

Her response put me in a quandary. While I loved the idea, I thought she might be a bit more hesitant, like me, thinking it a bit frivolous to drive three hundred miles just to see a concert. She wasn't helping me shoot myself down. Then, before I could respond to Pat he texted me back saying,

Well, I had to pull the trigger as tickets were available but few left together. Got us some nose bleeds (just like the old days) but they are together. Only $254 (not like the old days) Hah!

This sealed the deal for me. Pat mentioned he could sell the tickets if I couldn't make it which took the pressure off, but deep down, I wanted to go anyway. His ticket purchase made saying no almost impossible. Besides, as I said, I am a sappy nostalgic. As it turned out, I was able to schedule a book signing for one of my memoirs at a bookstore in downtown Saint Paul to make the trip a little more justifiable.

***

I arrived at Pat's house about 2:30 PM on the day of the concert. The show didn't start until 7:30, so it gave us a chance to catch up for a bit. I grabbed my suitcase out of the car along with a bottle of wine and a poinsettia I'd bought for Pat and his wife Laurie as a thank you for

hosting me for the night.

Pat met me in the driveway. He greeted me with a man hug, half handshake, half hug, and said, "Hey, good to see you, bro."

"Good to see you too, man," I replied.

Pat looked good. Over the years he'd put on some weight but seemed much trimmer than when I'd seen him last. Unlike my bald pate, he still had a full head of hair, albeit sprinkled with gray. Growing up we were both tall and slender. Thirty-eight years had changed us both physically, but we were both making the best of what we had. We'd both managed to stay married to our wives for over twenty-five years, so we had that going in our favor, as well. Unlike our years at

Cretin where girls and looks were all that mattered, it was good to be of an age where our wives accepted us and we were comfortable with the hand we were dealt with regards to our appearance. When it came right down to it, as friends, we were *still the same*, as Seger sings about in his song by the same name.

After we talked for a bit, we decided to go downtown early and get dinner before the show. We'd also heard about a pre-concert party hosted by KQRS radio at the arena where the show was, so thought that might be worth checking out. KQ was the station we'd grown up with, and had taken the contemporary hits of then, and was now playing them as the classic hits of today. They were touting "happy hour prices" for beer which piqued our interest in maybe hanging out with other fans for a bit.

When we arrived at the Xcel Energy Center arena we began looking for a place to park. In 1980 we saw Bob Seger at the now demolished Met Center. Tickets were twelve dollars and parking was four. I knew those days were long gone and would have been ecstatic to find a parking place for fifteen dollars to go along with our two hundred fifty-four dollars in tickets. So when Pat saw a lot across the street from the arena and said, "Hey, look thirty bucks to park there. Let's take it," I was a little dumbfounded.

"What? Thirty bucks? No way."

"I'll pay it. C'mon, Jim. Just do it. It's super convenient," Pat replied.

"Well, it is convenient, but, thirty bucks?"

"Hey, it's only six bucks more than the *tickets* cost us thirty eight years ago," Pat said with a laugh.

I laughed and shook my head at the crazy disparity between then and now. It's funny how time didn't make me any less a cheapskate than I was in 1980. Pat was always much freer with his money than I. It was one of his ways of showing friendship, by "treating" on a frequent basis. Knowing I wouldn't be able to counter his offer, plus anticipating the hassle of finding a different, less convenient parking spot, I took a left and turned into the lot.

We paid using Pat's credit card and walked to pick up our tickets at the Will-Call window. For some odd reason I'd saved every ticket stub from every concert I'd ever been to, so Pat made it a point to have us pick up our real tickets instead of using a "virtual ticket" on our smartphones. I wasn't sure but was hoping someone, somewhere, sometime might be impressed by my diligent ticket stub-hoarding over the years.

The Xcel Energy Center is a modern and beautiful facility. It sits on the footprint of the Saint Paul Civic Center, a venue I'd been to for multiple rock shows in the past, including that first concert experience with the Electric Light Orchestra in 1978. Knowing this made the significance of this show, in this place, even greater for me.

We found our way to the concourse level where the KQ party was held. It was a wide-open area with large speakers booming classic hits at levels that made talking difficult. I bought us both "happy hour priced" $7.00 Budweisers and we took a spot on the perimeter by the garbage can. There were twenty people milling about shouting over the music. All of them were over fifty years old, dressed in leather coats, cross trainers, Seger concert tees and other regalia indicative of the over-fifty crowd.

Pat took a swig of his watered down American pilsner, laughed and said, "I'm inclined to say this might be the lamest party I've ever been to. Everyone is so old."

"Ha! And you and I just might be some of them," I reminded him.

He laughed and said, "We can't be as old as some of these people. I mean they're OLD! Even the DJ is old!"

"Well, Seger's gotta be pushing seventy, so there's that," I said.

"True, but I've seen pictures and he doesn't look too bad for his age."

"Yeah, me too. He's aged better than Keith Richards."

"Everyone's aged better than Keith Richards," Pat said.

"That's for sure. To Seger and old friends!" I raised my beer in a toast.

Pat clinked his can to mine and we both took a swig. As much as we denied it, it felt good to be in my late fifties with a high school chum drinking an overpriced beer. It was a small piece of my past and a good chunk of my present all rolled up into one. At the same time, we didn't waste any time lingering at Saint Paul's lamest party. We worked quickly on our beers and talked about where to go for dinner. Fifteen minutes later we left unnoticed and made our way to Patrick McGoverns for a bite to eat.

***

After dinner, as we wove our way up toward the upper level seats inside the Xcel Energy Center, Pat again laughed and commented, "I just can't get over all the old people here."

"Yep, it's kinda eye opening, isn't it? But again, I reiterate, we might be a couple of them," I replied.

We stopped at the concession stand to get couple $11.00 beers. Another timeless certainty at any concert is overpriced alcohol. We'd had a couple at dinner and one at a packed tavern on our walk back to Xcel, so were feeling pretty good. Pat led the way to our seats high above the stage. It was still hard to fathom the seats cost a hundred and twenty-seven dollars each after all the various handling and "convenience" fees, but it beat the heck out of paying hundreds more for main floor seats. From a perspective standpoint, the seats were nearly identically as bad as the ones we'd purchased thirty-eight years before. Alas, it was the price one paid for an arena rock show.

The arena was still filling up as the warmup band, Larkin Poe, worked through some smoking blues rock tunes to prime the audience. They were a band fronted by two female guitarists. As they ripped through the classic hit, Black Betty, Pat leaned over and said, "I like these cats! They really rock it. You remember the time we saw the Stray Cats warm up for the Stones and they were almost booed off the stage?"

"Yeah. And look how well they ended up doing. That shows you what people know. These ladies are kickin' it!"

Pat and I always shared similar tastes in music, especially blues rock. In our teens and twenties music was an integral part of what bonded us together. We attended a lot of concerts together and our record collections were shared freely between one another. With our love of similar music, and our common faith in God, we were as tight as friends could hope for.

At intermission, we both found our way to the restrooms and Pat got himself another beer. We'd agreed that if I drove, he was allowed to let his hair down a little. Pat and I led fairly safe, nine-to-five lives as dads and husbands every other day of the year, so wanted to take advantage of the occasion to let loose a little bit and blow off some steam. In our youth we'd made blowing off steam an art form, so it felt good to be a little carefree for a night.

The crowd rose to its feet as Seger took the stage a little after 8:20. Neither Pat nor I recognized the opening song, but it didn't matter.

Pulled in by the music and the band we watched as Bob pranced and postured across the stage. He was old, as evidenced by his full head of gray hair, but he still had great energy and charisma.

As he and the Silver Bullet Band churned through the hits, I was taken back to the days of my youth. Songs like, "Still the Same," "Mainstreet," and, a personal favorite, "Turn the Page." That was the song I'd most wanted to hear Seger play in 1980 and he'd neglected to play it. When he played it this time I was ecstatic because it provided me with a little closure, as strange as that may seem. Seger's tour was called "The Final Tour," so the whole concert was a sort of chapter closing for both him and us, as fans.

When the first few notes of "Like a Rock" rang out, the crowd erupted. Pat leaned over and said, "This is it! Great song." The song was slow and melodic and the words were as meaningful as ever. Pat put his arm around my chair and gave me a man hug. I grabbed his hand and gave it a squeeze. We held hands for most of the song. It was both a strange and strongly moving moment. As wrong as it sounds and as awkward as it may have looked from the outside, for us it represented the culmination of over forty years of friendship. Something we never would have attempted during our years at Cretin for fear of being labelled. But here in this place, it was simply a point of great connection between two lifelong friends. He knew it, and I knew it. It was the pinnacle of an amazing two and a half hour concert, and a walk down memory lane.

***

With no real agenda planned, the next day, Pat and I agreed we would go to breakfast and then go out and shoot some pool. Back in our high school and college days, we spent many long hours, late at night, usually after the bars closed, having breakfast at Perkins restaurant. Our conversations on those nights were sometimes deep and reflective, sometimes light and fluffy, but always therapeutic. We talked about our faith, our families, girls and college. We discussed our dreams and fears, all while eating our late night breakfast and slurping down gallons of bad Perkins coffee.

This trip to Perkins in Roseville was no different. It was a running joke for years that Pat consistently ordered the Granny's Country Omelet while I always chose the Strawberry Rollups, a trio of crepes covered by a generous portion of strawberry compote and whipped cream. We stuck to the script this day as Pat ordered an omelet and I elected to get the Strawberry Croissant French Toast platter, the closest thing to the Strawberry Rollups I could find on the current menu. It seems some things are not sacred.

Over breakfast we talked about our lives, our work and our families. Both of us were successful in our careers and had raised decent, hardworking kids. At fifty-seven, we were at a point where we could look back at what we'd accomplished and marvel just for a moment about how we'd finally arrived. But it wasn't all happy talk. In the spirit of openness, we talked about the difficult periods too. Times of financial and job struggle as well as interpersonal issues we had with family and friends. These sessions around breakfast were equal parts psychotherapy and social catch-up. It was our way of working through some of the detritus of our past. While I was sitting there, I realized how much I missed it.

When we got ready to leave, as he often used to do, Pat intercepted the check and insisted on paying. It always made me feel guilty for not paying my share, but I also understood it was just Pat being Pat. His giving nature just never shut down and it was his way of saying let's do this again sometime.

***

We drove a couple of miles to Al's Billiards on Larpenteur Avenue. The venue had changed owners since I'd been there last in the early '80s. When I was a kid it was called Lee's Billiards. As we pulled into the lot, I laughed. The exterior of the place was *exactly* as I remembered it, with the exception of the name. It looked like Al had just ripped off the letters "EE" and replaced them with his name. He'd even re-used the capital 'L' of Lee's name, so it read AL's Billiards. Virtually nothing else had changed from the outside in the thirty-five plus years since I'd been there.

It was Pat's idea that we check our old haunt and play a few games. "Shooting stick" was one of our favorite things to do as teenagers and into our early twenties. Back then, it was an alcohol-free environment, so it was one of the places we could go and not have the temptation to imbibe, as it wasn't an option. It was just good clean fun. We did it often enough to become semi-accomplished players.

When we walked in, it was a bit like entering a museum of my past. The same ten tables sat in what looked like the exact same spots they were in when I had hair. Each table had a fluorescent light hanging above it and the counter was still near the front door, as it always was. The main hall was rimmed by bench seating and the center aisle had a couple of supporting pillars with small counters, cup holders and stools for a seat during those in-between shot spells. Near the restrooms, the classic record jukebox had been replaced by a fancy iTunes digital jukebox. It was probably the most noticeable change in the place.

I remember the original owner, Lee, as an ornery old cuss. He was tall and lean in his fifties with a military style crew cut, and an almost constant cigarette burning in an ashtray behind the counter. He used to shout from his seat, "Use the cup holders!" when we'd buy pop from the machine. If we managed to jump a ball off the table during a break or a difficult shot, he'd shout, "Easy! Keep 'em on the table!" It was pretty clear that even though we had a table half way across the floor, old Lee was holding roost and keeping his eye on us troublesome teens. He had moved his business from up the street into this new location and he was determined to keep it nice, even at the cost of a little adverse customer relations. After we got yelled at the first few times, we knew what not to do. We also knew it was just Lee's nature.

Pat checked in with Al and his wife and got a set of billiard balls. From behind the counter, Al flicked on the light over one of the tables near the back of the hall. The only other player there was an older guy playing alone a couple of tables away from the one we were assigned. I went and picked out a well-worn cue from the rack on the wall. I returned to the table and said, "How come I feel like I am holding what is likely the same cue I played with in the eighties?"

"Probably is," Pat said.

Pat racked them up and let me break. I crouched down, took aim, drew my cue back and let it fly. The balls caromed weakly off the bumpers in a maniacal pattern with none of them falling into a pocket.

"Crappy break," I said.

Pat laughed. "Yeah, I remember you used to say 'Feeble!' after a bad break. I think this qualifies."

"It sure does."

We took turns in futility for the first couple of shots, both of us rusty from lack of play. We laughed at each miss, just happy to be back circling the green felt displaying our mutual ineptitude. We both knew the reason we were here was to kill time, have some laughs and relive a bit of our past. Early on in our play it was clear we were doing that shrouded behind a very thin veil of billiard competency.

Everything about the place took me back to the days when my chemistry mid-term and how my hair was feathered were my biggest concerns. The only thing missing was a blaring jukebox. So, after the first game we wandered over to the iTunes machine on the far wall. At a dollar a song, the price was considerably more than the five songs for a buck back in the day. We put a couple of dollars in the slot.

"I've gotta play 'My Sharona.' That was one Dan played every time we came here," I said.

"Yeah, I remember that."

I punched on the keys searching for the mega-hit by The Knack. When I was finished Pat picked, "Rock and Roll Never Forgets," a Seger tune especially relevant given that we'd heard it live the night before. Here we were a couple of middle-aged nostalgics, reliving our past right down to the song and the place. It felt good.

The first notes of "My Sharona" thumped out triggering my thoughts of life at seventeen when my cares were few and my future was a gigantic unknown. It was those days, weeks and months before graduation where we'd come here just to forget about our jobs, our girl problems and our SAT scores.

But as I stood there, cue in hand and my best friend across the table strategizing his next shot, it became apparent my days at Cretin High School set the stage for the great life I'd been blessed with. Cretin provided me a quality education that qualified me for my college future at the University of Minnesota. That, in turn, led to a good job, which led to another, and another in an upward climb of success.

More importantly though, my days at Cretin had given me one really, really good friend. A lifelong companion. And while the rest of our core group of friends had lost contact, fallen away, relocated or intentionally distanced themselves, Pat and I had made it a point to stay in touch, albeit very loosely at times. I think it was because as gawky high schoolers we both recognized our similarities enough and knew it would sure help to have a listening ear to talk things through when times got tough. Someone you could share a pot of bad coffee with at Perkins as you laughed about "That time when…" Someone who could read your expression and anticipate your thoughts before they happened.

And if you get nothing else out of your high school experience other than one great friend, well, then I guess the rest is all worth it.

THE END

Cretin High Class of 1979

James Mark Acker
William Paul Alexander
Michael David Auran
Stephen Montgomery Baisch
David Paul Barnes
Callen Lee Beauregard
Donald Lawrence Belland
John Thomas Bergman
James Martin Berry
Michael William Bordenave
Robert William Brausen
Timothy Scott Bredahl
Patrick Joseph Brennan
Patrick John Breslin
Lawrence Peter Brown
Matthew Requa Caron
Kerry Frank Casey
David Matthew Chaffin
John Michael Chandler
James Christopher Cizek
Stephen James Clark
Timothy Edward Clasen
Terrence Patrick Coffey
Bernard Mark Colaizy
Christopher Brian Coleman
Ernest Randolph Companion
Timothy Mark Connelly
John Francis Coonan
Michael Gerard Costello
Mark Edward Cruz
James Matthew Cunningham
Dennis John Czech
James Wesley Dament
Joshua Jay Daniels
Mark Thomas Delaney
Daniel Anthony Dolan
Michael Thomas Dolan
Thomas Norris Doyle
Timothy Gerard Duffy
James Gerard Durand
Michael Raymond Fearing
Joseph Francis Ferraro V
Paul Brendan Flynn
Michael Edward Foley
Michael Allen Frederickson
Edward Jose Frias
Daniel Dominic Fritz
Patrick John Galatowitsch
Kevin Joseph Galligan
Thomas Richard Gautschi
Stephen Michael Gile
Gregg Lawrence Glaus
Timothy Charles Godfrey
Keith Allen Goldberg
Peter Carroll Grayson
Daniel James Gruber
Thor Halgren
Wayne Edward Hanrahan
Michael Jude Harris
Daniel Hamar Healy
Paul Joseph Heaney
Terry Joseph Hebl
David Michael Heller
Scott Robert Hennessey

Gilbert Paul Hernandez
Patrick Tanner Hewett
David Jude Hietpas
Bruce Lyman Hill
William Jules Hinchie
Christopher Patrick Hinze
Donald Stephen Horvath
John Joseph Hoye
Todd Joseph Jessen
Joseph John Joyce
Stephen Peter Joyce
Patrick Lawrence Judd
Brian Donald Kelm
Terrance James Kemp
James Michael King
Gregory Lee Kiwus
Mark Allen Krogh
Dominic Aaron Lagos
James Gerard Landwehr
Jeffrey Allen Lauth
Jack Morgan Lewis Jr.
John O'Hara Levau
Timothy Kennan Loney
Richard Neil Long
Jeffrey Peter Lotz
Daniel Thomas Lunney
Eugene Michael Lunney
Edward Robert Maas
John Francis Mangan
Robert Albert Martin
John Charles Mason
David John Mayer
Lawrence Edward McCallum
Brian Lawrence McCarthy
William Edward McClellan
Brian Patrick McConnon
Jamie Paul McDonell
John Ambrose McFarland
Robert Eldredge McGowan
William Albert Parranto
Edmund Charles Meisinger
Peter Phillip Meysembourg
James Charles Moliner
Steven Gerald Monson
Kieran Charles Moore
Michael Joseph Morgan
Jerome Walter Moynagh
John Francis Mueller
Michael Thomas Mulcahy
James Thomas Murphy
Patrick Martin Murphy
Kent Dion Murray
William Joseph Neuenfeldt
William Francis Nichols
Martin Donald Nistler
Kevin Peter O'Brien
Mark Gerald O'Brien
David John O'Neill
James Joseph Orfei
Thomas Robert Orput
David Cowper Parrish
Thomas Michael Perri
Darrick Anthony Perteet
Christopher Paul Peters

Jeffrey Tate Poston
David John Povolny
James Richard Prazak
Patrick Charles Prokop
Shawn Patrick Quinn
Peter Joseph Radermacher
John Russell Rask
Michael Edward Reardon
James Albert Reding Jr.
Thomas Joseph Reinartz Jr
William Patrick Robertson
Robert Alban Ruhland
Guy Matthew Rustad
John Vincent Ryan
Paul Joseph Ryan
Thomas Richard Sager
Steven Lawrence St. George
Joseph Earl St. Sauver
Michael Thomas Sausen
James Michael Schabert
Patrick Neil Schannach
Timothy Charles Schmid
Joseph Robert Schmitz
Thomas Lee Schroer
Philip Rorbye Schweitzer
Martin Joseph Sekevitch
Michael John Sheehan
Thomas Paul Skogseth
David Joseph Slattery
Brian Paul Sobaski
Michael Allen Sorenson
James Michael Staples
Andrew Joseph Stark
Michael Paul Stefanyshyn
Mark Joseph Steigauf
Craig John Swanson
James Lawrence Swanson
Richard Matthew Thomasser
James Joseph Thornton
Michael Anthony Tomars
Patrick Michael Towle
Thomas Gerard Traxler
Gary Joseph Trudeau
Ronald Timothy Tschida
Christopher John Tuckner
Daniel Patrick Turner
Michael John Van de Weghe
John William Voitn
Mark Anthony Waldron
Christopher George Walker
William Matthew Walsh III
Christopher Scott Ward
Douglas Arthur Weber
Gary Allen Weidell
James Michael Weiss
John Patrick Weiss
Robert Charles Welch
Gene David Wertheimer
Gregory Joseph Whaley
John Richard Wheeler
James Fleming Williams
Michael Anthony Woessner
Donald Gene Wright
Christopher Elliott Yorga
Paul James Zweber

186

ABOUT THE AUTHOR

Jim has two published memoirs, *Dirty Shirt: A Boundary Waters Memoir* and *The Portland House: A '70s Memoir*. He also has five poetry collections, *Thoughts from a Line at the DMV, Genetically Speaking, Reciting from Memory, Written Life,* and *On a Road*. His non-fiction stories have been published in *The Sun Magazine, Main Street Rag, Story News,* and others. His poetry has been featured in *Rosebud Magazine, Portage Magazine, The Orchards Poetry Journal,* and many others. Jim was the 2018-2019 poet laureate for the Village of Wales, Wisconsin and served as the nonfiction judge for the Jade Ring contest for the Wisconsin Writers Association in 2019. Jim lives in Waukesha, Wisconsin with his wife Donna, and works as a Land Information Systems Supervisor for Waukesha County. For more on his writing, visit: https://sites.google.com/view/jimlandwehr/home.

Made in the USA
Coppell, TX
03 August 2021

59914547R00105

"Jim Landwehr never disappoints, and Cretin Boy is no exception. This oftentim[es] hilarious, just as often poignant, journey captures the nostalgia of the late 1970s a[nd] mingles it with timeless examples of how every young person strives to reach adulthoo[d] Landwehr captures what makes us human at our weakest and at our best, in a way th[at] touches on the divine beauty of truth. A must read for your emotional journey, Cretin B[oy] will leave you deeply moved, and smiling."

—Summer Hanford, national and international Amazon best-selling author

Cretin High School, located in Saint Paul, Minnesota was a Catholic, all-male military academy that brought unique twists to the already difficult high school experience. Cretin Boys, as they were called, were subject to the oppression of both church and state as they navigated the diverse teaching styles of Christian Brothers, military instructors and lay teachers. *Cretin Boy* looks at those menial first jobs, takes you dancing with a girl at that first high school formal, and peels down the street in a Corvette-on-loan with a teen a[t] the wheel. It is a coming-of-age story with a military dress code, a coming-to faith story while smoking in the boy's room.

"A B-minus GPA from an all-male Catholic Military High School named Cretin does[n't] tell the whole story. With humor and insight, Jim Landwehr, shares his ups and down[s] dealing with high school. Not only that, he shares how those experiences shaped him[in] ways even better grades couldn't have."

--Bill Mathis, author of *Revenge is Necessary*, *The Rooming House Gallery*, *The Rooming House Diaries*, and *Face Your Fears*

"Military discipline and religious doctrine drilled into the cadets of Cretin High ea[ch] day lead the author down the traditional path to self. At the same time, testosterone, te[en] angst and the hedonistic pop culture of the 1970s bombard him with endl[ess] distraction. Ironic twists of the adolescent free-fall towards adulthood abound. Look[ing] for a slice-of-life story that nails the All-American Experience with humor, dra[ma] pathos, tension and struggle? I recommend *Cretin Boy*!"

--Robert Goswitz, author of *The Dragon Soldier's Good Fortune*.

Burning Bulb
PUBLISHING

9 781948 278287